PIVOT
To Present

Idea-rich strategies to deliver your virtual message with impact

Bob 'Idea Man' Hooey
Author of Speaking for Success!

Bob Hooey & friends share helpful tips and techniques

"You're muted!" or "Un-mute Yourself!"
2020's most used catch phrases

Our gratitude to my friends and colleagues who have generously shared their experiences, stories, lessons learned, tips, and techniques to assist each of us, 'me included', to better deliver our virtual message with more impact. This has allowed me to make this Idea-rich book more impactful for you. Much of what we share here works as well for business owners and salespeople who are now using this virtual medium to connect and help their clients. Many thanks!

My thanks as well to may amazing proofreader and editor, **Irene Gaudet**. She is my wife and a great support with my various adventures. BTW: **She offers this service to other authors.** Contact her about your book today... *igaudet@mcsnet.ca*

My thanks to my fellow Toastmasters and professional speakers around the world for adapting to this new virtual medium and encouraging me to follow their lead. You rock!

My thanks to the teachers who pivoted to help their students online and to support the parents homeschooling their own kids. To the parents who pivoted to teaching overnight. Wow!

You'll see some duplications and even some 'seemingly' contrary advice here... ☺ we encouraged sharing from their own experience. You'll also see a few excerpts from my revised 9th edition of **Speaking for Success!** to help with your presentation skills.

Visit our resources page:
www.SuccessPublications.ca/PIVOT.html

As we dig into our 'virtual' pivot

Pivot (noun) *A fixed point supporting something which turns or balances or a thing on which something else depends... (American Dictionary)*

Pivot (verb): *to change your opinions, statements, decisions, etc., so that they are different to what they were before: (Cambridge Dictionary)*

This word, pivot, was around long before COVID-19 hit; but it certainly found more wide-spread acceptance and its use expanded once we were locked down. We are not certain of when it became a world pandemic, and frankly that doesn't matter. It is and it has impacted us tremendously.

As I write and edit contributions for this latest book, we are still in a world-wide **COVID-19 pandemic**. Cities, states, and countries are in lockdown around the globe. Businesses are closed and workers are sitting at home, worried and waiting for it to work its way out (we hope!). Second waves are now hitting.

Governments are playing catch up, most having been caught totally unprepared, flat-footed, to lead and to cope with this global emergency. By the time it has worked its way out, millions will die. Not a fun scene, by any means.

Also important in this crisis are the long-range economic impacts of that shut down. No travel, little manufacturing, only essential businesses remain open (like groceries, pharmacies, hardware stores, etc.) This is a serious challenge for those of us in business if **we want to survive and stay in business over the long-haul.** And, we now have the time to work on it!

Disruption has changed our lives, both personal and corporate, as we know them! Overnight, businesses have shuttered their doors, laid off their staff, and turned off their lights. Overnight, businesses have had to pivot to survive.

Overnight, many workers and leaders have been thrust into the digital, virtually interconnected world. Working from home, in physical isolation, became our new norm. **How will we adapt and deal with this new global challenge?** The results are yet to be written and evaluated. But it is an exciting time too.

Quite simply, we don't know yet. We are making it up as we go along, feeling our way, one day at a time in totally unchartered territories. Some of us had already started down this virtual path of digital connection, collaboration, and creation. For others, just thrust into this digitally changing world, the results remain to be seen. More than ever, we need to work together to find our way in this confusing new world.

Suddenly being able to communicate, connect, and even conduct business in a virtual environment has become exceedingly important, even critical. We have had to **mentally pivot to explore new ways to do all these important actions**. I admit, I was a bit depressed when international engagements keep being postponed, canceled, or moved on-line. I had to get my mindset in adjustment that '**even though I was not able to travel, my ideas could**', and they have.

Like many of my speaking and training colleagues, I am exploring different ways to continue to deliver solid value to my clients – **digital ways to connect, educate, and engage**. My commitment to help my clients is as strong as ever, stronger, just the delivery methods have changed.

This is a very real challenge for our business owners, sales professionals, and many who were sent home, or are now working from home face every day. Many are looking at making a pivot to a new job or career as their previous one evaporated and will most likely not return, even when COVID-19 is under control.

"In challenging times people need HELP and they need HOPE! That is MY business!" Bob 'Idea Man' Hooey

One of the saddest challenges of Covid-19 are the thousands of people around the globe who cannot access the internet or barely access it. Am sure someone is working to find a way to provide cost effective access in this time of challenge.

More than ever, we need to reassess what business we are in, who are our potential clients, and how we can best reach and serve them despite these disruptive times.

More than ever, we need to learn how to reach out and connect and communicate with those who are important to us: our families, our friends, our colleagues, our clients.

Those who take this seriously and adapt will emerge stronger, perhaps, totally redesigned, and restructured. And, perhaps more relevant and profitable as well. This is our opportunity, our challenge as business leaders, to demonstrate our commitment to our clients, teams, suppliers, and communities.

We can do it by working together! We can do it by sharing our lessons and encouragement in moving online and moving forward. That is why I created PIVOT to Present.

I reached out to some of my amazing colleagues in the speaking industry for their current tips, techniques, stories, and lessons learned as they pivoted to presenting and communicating online. I've compiled their contributions in this book, along with my own thoughts and experimentation.

You will find some repetition in the ideas shared. These have been left for a simple reason: reinforcement of something that is true from the applied wisdom of many.

We have set up an online resource page as well and welcome submissions you feel might be of value to your fellow readers. **www.SuccessPublications.ca/PIVOT.html**

Bob 'Idea Man' Hooey, *Creative Lead*
Certified Virtual Presenter

Table of Contents

As we dig into our 'virtual' pivot..3

Table of Contents 6

How to Present & Teach in the Virtual World.............................8

What do we mean by…?..15

The Big Tech Reset 17

New Energy for The New Stage 19

Speaking into a black hole 21

Continuing to learn together - virtually 22

Presenting online..23

Getting Started – a simple approach..24

Three Key Ideas To 'Successful' Speeches 25

My little 'grain de sel'..28

Presenting in a digital environment to international groups.....29

Lights, Camera, Wait… What? Lights? 33

Learning from Sesame Street 36

Can you see me now?..38

The Bitter Pill 'The Speaking Profession' Needs to Swallow...39

A few reminders to effectively present on-line 41

Meeting tips for different types of virtual technology 42

I Lost My Voice 47

Foundations for Speaking Success!..49

Kudos to Toastmasters International..60

Getting started presenting on-line..61

Studio tips..62

Mastering your virtual meeting presence - Top 3 pro tips for upping your game 63

Judging perspectives 68

Kudos to our amazing teachers and parents who are helping educate the leaders of tomorrow 70

Julie's gems… 71

Always have a backup plan, or two 72

Ideas To 'Handle' Your Nervousness 73

Valda's suggestions 75

A few more tips… 77

Lessons learned presenting virtually 78

Virtual meetings and interviews 79

Tips for connecting better with your online audience 80

Retail pivot – great idea to connect and sell 81

Humour and writing tips 82

Using Humor… A Few Safety Tips 103

A few tips from Terry 105

[Renaming game] 107

Guides for giving an effective virtual presentation 109

My Journey to Running Online Summits 110

A few final ideas from Bob… 114

What they say about Bob 'Idea Man' Hooey 115

Bob's Publications 117

Copyright and License Notes 119

Acknowledgements and disclaimers 120

Thanks for reading PIVOT To Present 122

How to Present & Teach in the Virtual World

Patricia Fripp teaches how to connect with your audience when you present and teach virtually.

Editor's note: *I decided to begin our mutual exploration and learning with some wise words from my amazing friend and colleague as she gives us a great overview of this new medium. She was gracious in allowing us to include this section.* ***Patricia Fripp*** *is a Hall of Fame keynote speaker, executive speech coach, sales presentation skills consultant, and online learning expert. In Ms. Fripp's career, she has delivered over 3,500 presentations as well as countless virtual presentations, ahead of the curve.*

Business and educational professionals know that whenever you present, whether you're talking to one person or one hundred, you want to connect with your audience and get your message across. **What's the best way to do this when you deliver a virtual presentation?**

These strategies will help you get your message across, maximize your impact, and catch and keep the attention of remote students and audiences when you present or teach virtually.

Before You Present

Nothing happens without first understanding the technology.

Educational and business entities use different technologies. They include **Zoom, WebEx, GoToMeetings, and Teams**. Even a seasoned presenter, who is superb at delivering live presentations, can find the shift nerve-racking.

Become familiar with your system. Make sure your environment is tidy behind you. If you use Zoom, you can upload images that can be branded to your organization. However, you must have a green screen behind you. If you do not, you will often disappear into the background when you move.

Invest in a professional microphone to improve the sound.

Let there be light! Depending on the room you are delivering from, you will be best served if your window is in front of you.

Depending on the time of day that light changes. Invest in additional lights.

The best connection will be wired. If you have a wireless connection and a large audience, you will have more problems.

Before you present, **close every open program and application you are not using on your computer**. Presenting virtually requires a large amount of bandwidth.

If you work from home, negotiate with family members so that they will stay offline and not stream videos while you present.

In the Beginning

Use looping slides. Once your audience tunes in, how do you make sure they are entertained and feel involved even before the program begins? A series of looping slides is the best way to welcome virtual audiences to your webinars.

Looping slides are a great way to convey important information and keep attendees entertained while they're waiting for your presentation to begin.

These slides should communicate the following: when the session will begin; the conference dial-in number; your photo, name, and title; what the audience is going to learn; and what to do in case of problems.

You can also include quotes about the content they will be learning.

Your other option is to open the meeting early. This way your audience or students can greet you, ask questions in the chat, or tell you where they are from. Naturally, you have the option of doing both.

Think Hollywood! Be creative in your use of visual appeal. In a live presentation, you would tell stories and give specific examples. In a web presentation, you'll need even more visuals to engage the audience.

Use more slides than you would in a face-to-face presentation. An easy way to do this is to reveal bullet points one at a time as you bring them up, rather than all at once before you discuss them. This is a "build" in your PowerPoint. Using mostly visuals and little text is even better. Keep it simple, keep it moving, and interact often.

Build Your Presentation

Plan your structure. Outline your presentation on paper, whiteboard, or flip chart before you build the PowerPoint presentation. The creative process is messy.

Your PowerPoint and visuals are tidy. It's better to have fewer points and illustrate them well.

Be sure to cover these steps:

Introduce your learning objectives.

Reinforce the benefits of knowing this information.
Explain the agenda and timing of your session. When will you include Q&A and interaction?

Add any logistics and explain how your students and audience will interact with you. Incorporate polls, chats, the interactive tools associated with your platform.

Welcome Your Audience

Turn on your webcam to welcome your audience. If you want to turn it off while you interact with the slides, fine. Turn it back on, however, to answer questions, to let them know what action to take next, and to thank them at the end for their attention and interest.

The purpose of your opening is to **arouse interest in your subject.** Open with a grabber slide, a visual that will grab your audience's attention. Then, "Welcome to . . ." (the event, class, or learning experience).

Start with a Strong Opening

After the grabber slide and the welcome, **it's up to you to engage the audience immediately** with a powerful and relevant hook that includes the word "you."

A catchy fact: "It may interest you to know that . . ."

A startling statistic: "Would it surprise or shock you to know . . ."

An intriguing challenge: "Nine months ago you enrolled in … You are now in the exciting position to …"

Strong openings grab your audience's attention, and then it's up to you to keep it. It's less effective to start with "Good morning," than it is to say, "Welcome! You are in for a treat! You are about to learn …"

As you introduce the session, **sell the listeners** on how they're going to benefit. Keep them glued to their screen. The world is full of students and adults with short attention spans.

Introduce yourself next. Only after you've sold the session should you introduce yourself (unless someone else will be introducing you). Do not introduce yourself first. You'll need to say something your listeners care about before they will care who you are.

Forge an Emotional Connection

Use a high "I vs you" balance. The most powerful communication combines both intellectual and emotional connections. An intellectual connection appeals to educated self-interest with data and reasoned arguments. Emotion comes from engaging the listeners' imaginations, involving them in your illustrative stories by frequent use of the word "you," and answering the unspoken question, "What's in this for me?"

For example, don't say, "I'm going to talk to you about presentation skills." Instead say, "In the next 56 minutes, you will learn the six secrets of making every presentation a success; the four benefits of effective presentations in your careers; and the three mistakes most speakers make until they know what you are about to learn."

Build in interaction. Depending on the technology you use for your web training and the format of your class or program, make sure you interact with the audience when it's most logical.

A simple method is to find that logical place and time, then stop and ask, "Based on what you have heard so far, what are your questions?

Use memorable stories. People rarely remember your exact words. Instead, they remember the mental images that your words evoke. Support your key points with vivid, relevant stories. Help them make a movie in their heads by using memorable characters, exciting situations, dialogue, and humor. With a combination of your examples and visuals, it will be a memorable presentation.

Use effective pauses. Good music and good communication both contain changes of pace, pauses, and full rests. Pauses mark the time when your listeners think about what they have just heard. If you rush on at full speed to cram in as much information as possible, chances are you will lose your listeners.

It's okay to talk quickly, but whenever you say something profound or important or ask a rhetorical question, pause.

Avoid Filler Words

Avoid filler words: "Hmm, ah, er, you know what I mean?" In webinars and virtual meetings, filler words sound even more prominent than in person. Are you using them? Why not get in the habit of rehearsing and recording your presentations? Review the replays of past sessions. After all, you can't improve on what you are unaware of.

As the actor **Michael Caine** has said, **"Rehearsal is the work; performance is the relaxation."**

Before Your Closing

Review and assume that your audience will have questions as you present. As with an in-person presentation, always review your key ideas with a virtual audience before concluding.

Then ask, "Before my closing remarks, what questions do you have?"

Tell them what to do next. Emphasize what the audience should do once the virtual training is over. Be clear what their next logical steps should be. Send them off energized, focused, and ready to take action.

End on a high note.

Your last words linger. Your final comment must be memorable and must reinforce your main message. An example is, "Remember, there is no greater skill than . . ." Or, as I often do, "Remember, habits are like railway tracks. They take a long time to put into place. When there they will take you anywhere you want to go." Your last words will stay with your audience. Make sure they are your own. Make sure they are powerful and don't quote anyone else.

When you excel in virtual presentations and webinars, and you will reinforce your reputation as an expert. Good luck. Remember, your last words linger!

Patricia Fripp, CSP, CPAE, *Cavett recipient*, _www.fripp.com_
Included with permission

I include this following quote as Patricia has mastered this key skill. I've been on the receiving end of some of her questions.

"When it comes to the design of effective learning experiences, one **provocative question** *is worth a hundred proclamations."*
Bernard Bull

Visit our resources page:
www.SuccessPublications.ca/PIVOT.html

What do we mean by...?

A few quick definitions to ensure you are on the same page with us. My friend Antoni kindly provided his virtual e-manual with permission to use whatever we thought would help. We will also have the full manual on our PIVOT resource page. www.SuccessPublications.ca/PIVOT.html

Video meetings

Where you each have a camera and you can all see each other. Everyone can join the conversation. Zoom is one platform.

Phone meetings

Where you only hear each other. These days, it's often Skype without webcam. Everyone can be in on the call.

Webcast

For example, YouTube or Bambuser. Some are gathered together, some are scattered. Not everyone can participate on the same terms.

Webinar

Like a virtual cinema... a seminar delivered over the Internet. One is talking, the rest – scattered – can watch (or at least listen). The chat function can be used, as well as video – up to a point. Zoom can be used in this manner.

Shared desktop

Where everyone in the virtual meeting can share PowerPoint slides, virtual whiteboard, etc.

Synchronous communication

Online here-and-now communication. A 'live' meeting.

Asynchronous communication

Online>offline>online – for example, e-mail or voicemail. (Back in time: letter, telegram or fax.)

excerpted Virtual Meetings by **Antoni Lacinai, CVP** *&* **Mike Darmell** www.lacinai.se *Included with permission*

Other designations within the speaking industry

CVP: Certified Virtual Presenter

CSP: Certified Speaking Professional (NSA/GSF)

CPAE: Council of Peers Award of Excellence (NSA)

AS: Accredited Speaker (Toastmasters)

HoF: Hall of Fame (CAPS)

WCPS: World Champion of Public Speaking (Toastmasters)

Cavett: The highest award given by the National Speakers Association

Spirit of CAPS: The highest award for service given by the Canadian Association of Professional Speakers, now named after Warren Evans, one of our founding fathers.

The Big Tech Reset

David is a tech guru as well as a CAPS colleague. Thanks my friend.

2020 has been an interesting year, so far. Many feel there was a big reset button pressed on everything in life. As the new normal is emerging, we are discovering communication with family, friends, and for business is taking new shape. Many people scrambled to get their technology back to a reasonable working level in terms of video conferencing capabilities. This means good quality video (webcam), solid audio (microphone), reliable connection (Internet), and decent bones running the communication software (fast laptop or desktop).

Zoom has become a verb implying connecting with people by video, though several are using it for audio only as well. Many wonder **which platform is the best**: Zoom vs Google Meet (Hangouts) vs Microsoft Teams vs Cisco WebEx vs Skype ...

Use the platform your clients/family/friends are most comfortable with. Good customer service in business and how you get new clients is by making things as easy as possible for them and solving their problems. Don't force your technology upon someone else if they seem apprehensive. Yes, we all think "our" solution is so easy, but many *fear the unknown*. This is one more roadblock for them becoming a potential new client or contact of yours.

When someone agrees to a virtual meeting, send them a calendar invite that includes the video link. Provide everything to them on a silver platter so it is as easy as possible. Ensure you are on time, and you are professional. This includes what your own camera is viewing: good lighting, reduce background distractions, what you are wearing, the quality of your video and audio. Ensure your Internet connection goes well for the video session and consider connecting your device with a wired ethernet cable to your Internet router instead of

Wi-Fi. Make sure others in your household aren't watching Netflix at the moment which congests your connection to the Internet and will make your video & audio lower quality. Test any changes you make; this is easy by having a quick session with a friend or colleague before your important meeting.

With the constant advancements in technology, it is recommended to **be part of a group such as a mastermind**. This trusted group of peers is great for asking questions, brainstorming, keeping up on the latest tips & tricks, and giving feedback. They can be the ones who help, recommend and test new technologies. Have a regular monthly Zoom session with your group that is always carved away in your calendar. For your first session, have everyone bring one single tip they would think everyone should know such as a website, an app, a gadget, or any life hack. Keep it brief and fun.

David Papp, *P.Eng. www.davidpapp.com Included with permission*

Certified Virtual Presenter/CVP

You may see this designation behind the names of some contributors; more as it becomes known. This is an indication that they have been tested (by e-Speakers) with a standardized on-line test to ensure they have the necessary equipment, skills, and expertise to present effectively in this exciting new medium.

This is a new designation created following the outbreak of COVID-19 around the globe. Our guess is it will be soon an industry standard in this new medium. **www.espeakers.com**

Zoom.com has amazing tutorials… use them!

New Energy for The New Stage

I first met Graeme at one of our GSF events where we were both speaking, and we reconnected again when I accepted an invite to keynote at the PSA SA event in Cape Town. Graeme organized a wine tasting afternoon for many of our international speakers and played host. Generous man and friend. He is a brilliant man who wisely choses his words and ideas.

Like many speakers, I am an introvert. People who only see us speakers on big stages in front of large audiences might not believe that many of the world's top speakers do not get their energy from being with people (that's the correct definition of introverts and extroverts - it's not your ability to engage with people, but rather about where you get your energy from; and introverts get it from being alone).

Some speakers - and most entertainers - thrive on audience response and the 'energy in the room' - they're extroverts. This is particularly true, for example, of stand-up comedians. There's a wonderful moment in a good set where the laughter of some of the people in a room sets off everyone else, and the whole venue just resounds with people sparking each other's enjoyment. That's why comedians prefer smaller venues with low ceilings (I'm serious - they do). These speakers and entertainers must be finding the new virtual world hard.

On the other hand, I have been preparing my whole life for Lockdown.

And here is the one thing introverts know that everyone needs to learn to be successful in virtual presentations: you must bring your own energy to the new stage. **Your stage is now your computer, webcam, green screen, studio, lighting rigs, and whatever other equipment you've bought to set yourself up** (see other sections of this book for practical assistance on this).

But once it's 'go time' and all you have is you and that little green dot that indicates your camera is live, you must bring all the energy required to make your session come alive. I really do think that those of us who are used to managing our own energy very carefully are better prepared for this than extroverts and the big personalities in our industry.

So, here are **three things I've learnt** about this that will hopefully help you:

1. **Think like a radio presenter and speak to one person only.**

There is something intimate about radio, and good radio DJ's know just how to use their voices to connect with the listener. **Listener - singular!** Remember that your audience is also sitting at home, alone, without a crowd around them. So, as you present, you might see 20, 50, 100 or even a 1,000 people logged in, but **each of them is experiencing you alone.** You need to speak to them showing sensitivity to that context and experience.

2. But, possibly paradoxically, you have to **bring your big stage presence to that small screen.**

An intimate conversation with a big stage presence. It is a paradox, and you must work out what it means for you. But getting this balance right is the secret. I do it with a combination of my voice (one on one), eyes (looking directly at the camera most of the time), facial expressions (big stage) and my use of the space (I stand and use the 'leaning into the camera' move to speak one on one with people).

3. **Exaggerate the changes of pace, tone, and cadence of your presentation often.**

Good speakers do this normally, but you need to emphasise it even more in this virtual world. Fast bits need to be even faster, with longer pauses and contrasts with slow bits. We often think of being loud, but don't forget to be soft too. To get all this right, you need great equipment, most important of which is a top end microphone that can pick up the nuances of your voice. Don't skimp on your mic purchase.

We have a new virtual stage. We need to learn how to bring new energy to that stage to be successful in the new world we are now in. This world will last a long time too.

Even when physical meetings start again, there will be a lot of hybrid events, and as speakers we might have opportunities to present virtually forever. It is worth developing the skills to do this as best you can.

Dr. Graeme Codrington, *CSP, PSAE, SAHOF, CVP*
www.graemecodrington.com Included with permission

Speaking into a black hole

Ever felt like you were talking to a black hole and wondered if anyone even was listening? I did recently, when I was delivering some training to Track and Field officials across Canada. The host asked everyone to turn off their video and audio to conserve band width. The silence was defening.

As my husband says, very much like speaking on TV when you speak directly into the camera and hope there is someone viewing.

If you can, have someone in your viewing audience so you can see a bit of reaction. If that is not possible, perhaps put a picture next to your camera of people smiling or even laughing, so that you can get the energy from them.

Irene Gaudet, *www.VitrakCreative.com Included with permission*

Continuing to learn together - virtually

I have attended many of the Thurs. Biz Accelerator evenings. Wow! I find them valuable and enjoy the interaction with colleagues. Thanks John!

On March 14th, 2020, the **National Speakers Association** in Las Vegas held our monthly meeting. Two days later the state of Nevada issued stay at home orders. Covid-19 confined us to our homes and shut down our businesses. We had no idea how long it would last. We were thinking a week or two, maybe a month at most. (oops)

This happened in the middle of my year as chapter president. I looked forward to connecting with my friends at our NSA meetings and now even that was in jeopardy. I knew I could not be the only person in need of connection.

The bright side to being locked up at home was several projects I had wanted to get done to improve my business would finally get done. Being a part of the NSA community exposes me to new ideas and helps to keep me accountable to get things done. The day after the stay-at-home orders were issued, I organized a Thursday evening Zoom meeting. The meeting was intended to bring everyone together, check in to see how everyone was doing, and to keep each other motivated to continue working. It would also be a good opportunity to get to know a little more about one another and our businesses. It succeeded!

We have not missed a Thursday night meeting since that first Zoom call on March 19th. We bring in experts from around the world to help make our individual businesses better. I've since passed on the presidential baton, but the leadership committee has no intention of stopping our Thursday night virtual meetings. We have used this pandemic as an opportunity to get to know each other better and to grow our businesses.

John Polish, *Certified Virtual Presenter, www.johnpolish.com*

Presenting online

I met Charlotte when we went to Cape Town for PSA SA. She and her husband, Richard welcomed us into their home prior to the convention.

Before we present anything, on any platform, we must **focus on the outcome we want**. It may be that we want people to watch us and think that we are clever or funny. It may be that they should watch us and be impressed with our skills and proficiency with online technologies. Or it may be that our intention is to impress a message onto the hearts or minds of an engaged audience and give them a reason to consider taking some action.

All of these outcomes have a place, but assuming as professional speakers and presenters, that our primary goal in most of our presentations, is to serve the audience and the client, then we must ensure that our use of technology serves us, and not the other way around.

As professionals, it is imperative that we master our technologies, regardless of whether we present in person or online. But sometimes, especially when we are new to a platform or have discovered a cool new feature, we allow that technology to take centre stage.

We all grew up and moved away from the zooming and whirling Power Point animations and stopped making our audiences motion-sick. But when we discover a cool new trick, like video green screen backgrounds, or Prezi zooming out to big pictures, or live polls, or animated avatars, we can't help ourselves but play with them. And we should.

We should know how they work and what is possible so that we can serve the audience and the message where appropriate. But the technology should never be centre stage.

Just like a good speech, that is so well rehearsed that it doesn't sound rehearsed at all, we should be so proficient with the technologies we choose to use, that only our most clued up and experienced colleagues should even be aware of how we just reinforced our message with the use of some technological feature.

If our **primary goal is to serve the audience and the client**, then we want the audience to remember the message first, the messenger second and to spend only a passing thought for the medium.

Charlotte Kemp, *SdPFA*, *www.charlottekemp.co.za Included with permission*

Getting Started – a simple approach

Getting started online has gotten easier in the past year. Zoom has always had a free program which can be used to learn the ropes before you invest in professional programs.

Zoom Personal Meeting - Free
- Host up to 100 participants
- 40-minute maximum group meetings
- Unlimited 1:1 Meetings

If you have a laptop, most of them have a microphone and camera so you're good to go, for now. As you move forward you can invest in reasonably priced HD cameras and plug in mics. But, for now you can experiment by hosting calls with family and friends to learn the program and become more proficient in leveraging it professionally. Zoom has some amazing demo videos to help you get started; invest your time to learn. *I use Zoom for client interviews, and it worked great with my District leaders when I was a Region Advisor. I was comfortable, but still needed to learn how to present in this new medium.* **Jump in the water online is fine.** ☺

Three Key Ideas To 'Successful' Speeches

Whether you are preparing to present virtually or in a live event there are certain points or foundations that help ensure you present with power. These are some I know work and have shared freely around the globe, in some cases virtually from my home office.

The cardinal rule to being effective in public speaking is **"NEVER BE BORING!"** But how do we do this when we are nervous and under *pressure to perform*?

I've been teaching my clients and various in-person classes that the **"three key ideas to speaking success"** are based on acquiring the knowledge you need to successfully capture their attention, to connect with your audience, and to achieve your shared objectives.

 **Those three key ideas to speaking success are:**

KNOW your subject or topic
KNOW your audience
KNOW yourself

If you **know your subject** and are thoroughly prepared, you will be much more relaxed and effective than if you are just 'winging' it.

Taking time to organize and delve into your topic will give you a sense of the depth you bring to the platform. It will also give you much more information than you will be able to deliver, which gives you back-up information for additional presentations and questions. This confidence, based on acquired knowledge, works wonders in helping to keep the "butterflies flying in formation," as we used to say in Toastmasters.

If you **know your audience**, you will be better prepared to effectively analyze their needs and select from the body of knowledge you've acquired on your topic to serve or solve those needs; to actually present something that is relevant and helpful to them.

The better you know or *understand* their backgrounds, history, connections, education, gender, and their ages; the better you will be able to construct and deliver your presentation in a way that is interesting, relevant, and informative to them.

If you **know yourself**, you can draw on your own experiences and build on your own strengths in developing your own 'unique' speaking style.

You can share your own ideas and 'unique' stories in a way that allows you to be most effective. Self-knowledge is a tool of effective and successful communication.

Continually ask yourself, ***"If I was in the audience, why would I be interested in this point or topic?"*** Then simply make sure you have a good answer for that question. Your audiences are people, just like you.

The better you know yourself, the better equipped you are to effectively reach them.

By skillfully combining your knowledge of self, your subject, and your audience, you will effectively increase your impact. You will also expand your impact as a presenter, interviewee, or speaker.

A final note here:

Be sure to apply the **3 P's of public speaking – PREPARATION, PRACTICE, and PERFORMANCE!**

There is no substitute for being prepared, by practicing until you are certain that you are ready to present your material in a confident manner. Anyone who says they just get up and *fake it* is leading you down the wrong path. Prepare, practice, and polish and then, confidently walk on stage and *play* with the audience. That is what I've learned, and it works well for me.

The master's *only* make it look easy. They have put in the time, (*lots of it*) far from the public eye, long before they are introduced... and it shows!

Share your dreams, take some risks!

Bob 'Idea Man' Hooey, excerpt from Speaking for Success! Used with permission www.ideaman.net www.successpublications.ca

 **PRO-tip: "Tech Tips - Be prepared!** *(These make sense if you are presenting virtually as well.)* If using a laptop, ensure all updates are applied before you begin and reboot more than once to be sure. Avoid the embarrassment of a forced lengthy update occurring when you try to begin. Show up early (log in) and test your connections at the venue or on-line platform.

Always have a backup plan as Murphy strikes when you least expect it. This can include spare batteries, different adapters to connect to older projectors and audio splitters, longer extension cables, a speaker, a copy of your slide deck on a USB stick or when all tech fails, a printout of your slides."

David Papp, P.Eng., www.davidpapp.com Included with permission

My little 'grain de sel'

Claire and I met and began our friendship in Manila last year when we both keynoted the Philippines Association of Professional Speakers event as well as an HR event the next day. She was part of my Speakers Roundtable this April when we pivoted to produce it online instead of a 2-day live event in Barcelona. We have share virtual stages as well, including her virtual book launch in September of this year.

I think the strangest thing about speaking virtually is you don't necessarily see the other side. When you are live you can see people watching you or falling asleep but when there is no return it's when you start questioning yourself whether or not you are making an impact to those people watching you.

I have always said to myself if I can impact one person in the audience today, I would be happy. So, I do the same, I have actually cut a photo of someone and stuck the photo around my camera, so when I speak I have someone I speak to and I feel closer to the audience because I speak to that one photo and so hopefully the others who are listening feel the same emotions when I talk as I speak to a real person now, who is in front of me....

Live or virtual, I always prepare myself as if I was in a ball of sunshine, so I build myself up with lot of sun, shining energy and I know this will also reflect in the way I present...

Claire Boscq-Scott, *Certified Virtual Presenter,*
www.claireboscqscott.com Included with permission

"Online learning is not the next big thing; it is the now big thing."
Donna J. Abernathy

Presenting in a digital environment to international groups

Gijs is a friend and colleague who is a covid-10 survivor. He came back in time to help us pivot from our two-day LIVE Barcelona event to our virtual one. He brings a wealth of wisdom to the stage or the monitor.

A Corporate Trainer sits on a small (home) office in in a town on the Eastern border of the Netherlands. It is very early in the morning. The streets are quiet, the birds are just starting to move a little and there is a quiet mood hanging over the streets. With practiced hand he checks and rechecks his screens, sound settings, lightning, and backup systems.

He logs in, does a final adjustment, and then uses Zoom in combination with Webinar Geek and Mentimeter to address, captivate and enchant his audience.

Under the calm demeanor and easy patter, he is nervous. It is the first time that his client has entrusted him to work on a remote session with the branch offices in Shanghai, Mumbai, and Doha simultaneously. Today, the client who is based out of Milan cannot attend the session and has turned over the control to our intrepid presenter.

The session gets underway but soon there is a problem which starts being felt. No matter the easy-going, friendly demeanor of the presenter or the calm, collected, factual approach interspersed with personable humor, there is very little audience interaction. No matter what he tries, he just cannot seem to connect properly. The seconds tick by ever more slowly, the minutes loom like concrete checkpoints and the 45-minute session now takes on a distorted sense of Orwellian drama. Our Trainer starts wondering whether this really is the job for him yet is desperately nervous about his client's response.

With the advent of digital speaking, training, and consulting and with the ever-increasing global reach of our work it is essential that we look beyond the technical and presentation skills training that we are used to. We need to become fully aware that reaching out to global audiences will inevitably mean that our messages and offerings will be weighed on the cultural scale of our audiences. Failure to account for this can be frustrating for all parties at best and career killing at worst. We need to understand our audiences, reach into their collective programming, and start playing the musical instruments of their choice rather than laying down the ground rules as we have learnt them.

The corporate trainer would do well to spend a significant amount of time in preparing for his presentation in laying down the fabric and tapestry for dealing with international groups.

As our borders expand, we realize that though there are similar stories, requirements, hopes, aspirations and dreams across cultures, the way we share and interpret those is different. Like multicolored strings and patterns, **the way each culture weaves their tapestry is different.**

Which aspects should we focus on, and which aspects should we investigate? I think there are several.

We should start off by looking at the communication styles that are used by your target country or even company. Do they communicate very directly, are they fact based and consider "truth" to be more important than diplomacy? Do they communicate with passion, full of gestures and drama, do they tend to speak out of turn and interrupt yet keep a conversation going at multiple levels? Do they tend to listen very carefully, seem very diplomatic and resist giving direct answers, choosing diplomacy almost at the expense of "truth"? Understand and adjust to that style.

After that it is essential to look at how the audience views leadership. What stories do that culture tell us of brave men and women? Are they lone heroes, einzelgängers (independent, maverick), generals on horseback, directing the armies at their feet or are they the quiet leaders who facilitate, lead from a position of influence and trust? Adjust your training and speaking for maximum impact.

Next, we should look at the way our target audience looks at interaction. Is this a culture that values the individual or the group more? Is there a tendency for lone warriors or is interaction required from an early age? Do the people belong to and feel comfortable in groups or prefer solitary interactions and dreams?

What is the attitude to work like? Does one live to work or is work a "necessary evil" and is the focus on intrapersonal relationships? Is it more important that the work gets done irrespective of the length of time you have to be present or is the mental and social wellbeing of the individuals put first? In understanding this we can understand where we lay our focus on as trainers, speakers, and consultants.

How does your audience view risk-taking? Is it something that is generally accepted are their heroes seen as great not because of their trials and tribulations but despite them? Are mistakes accepted, analyzed, and acted upon or vilified, frowned upon and forgotten?

The stories that your audience shares with each other will give you some insights into whether the audience and culture are focused on the long term or whether they are at ease with acting quickly, seizing opportunities as they arise with nary-a-care for whether there is a golden thread to the future that runs through their decision-making.

How does your audience feel about rewarding themselves? Do they feel comfortable in granting themselves rewards and gifts or do they feel the work is never done? Is the journey end and the story conclusion that of a beach holiday with all the trimmings or does the central character always return straight to the dessert because they are always-on, never done?

Are the companies that we reach out to people oriented or task focused? **Are they living their own mottos and building their legacies?** When viewing the websites but also when talking with the individuals concerned, we can learn a lot and use this to let our stories resonate, entwine, comfort, encourage and uplift. If we understand our audiences and are humble enough to walk in their shoes whilst we are sharing with them.

We really need to look at the heroes, symbols, and rituals that our target audience holds dear. We need to research them, understand, and dissect them and in our own way mix these together with our personal stories, our professional skills and our heartfelt feeling of hope to create beautiful story images and speaking tapestries to bring light to every far-flung corner of the globe.

Get used to reading authors like Hofstede, Minkov, Schein, Meyer, Lewis, Katz, and Kramer. Incorporate some of the lessons they have taught on Cultures, Organizations, Structures and Anthropology. Read their works with a view to understanding the incredibly rich tapestry against which your potential clients live, breathe, and operate internationally.

Your audiences, your soul and ultimately your wallet will thank you for it.

Gijs Hillmann, *International Corporate Trainer www.gyshillmann.com*
Included with permission

"We need to bring learning to people instead of people to learning."
Elliot Masie

Lights, Camera, Wait... What? Lights?

Darren and I are both Accredited Speakers and have been friends and colleagues for many years, even sharing a stage or two along the way. He is a World Champion of Public Speaking (Toastmasters International) He is an amazing talent who invests in his craft and has helped 1000's of speakers hones theirs. Thanks for sharing, Darren.

Hollywood is famous for the line, **"Lights, Camera, Action!"** But your home studio is not Hollywood! However, we need to make it a priority to look professional. If you are presenting as an expert or emerging expert online, you need to up your lighting game. Don't stress, it's simpler than you think.

If you want to look like a professional, you've got to approach this as a professional. What are the basics? Can they see you and can they hear you? Pretty simple? **Then why do most people not look good in their home studios on Zoom?** Because then never took the time to figure it out. Let that not be you! Let that not be a mistake you make. Focus.

If you are look at upgrading your home studio now, feel very fortunate. Its easier and more affordable now than just a few years ago. I had been making YouTube videos and doing Zoom calls for years. For many years I used a light kit with lights that got really hot, required bulbs that weren't adjustable. I ended up getting a simple dimmer switch for $10 at Home Depot that helped. If you do use lightbulbs, I highly recommend getting a dimmer switch or two. If your home studio is like mine, **the natural light changes as the daylight changes.**

The coolest thing is you can set up your own zoom meeting, by yourself and experiment. Don't overcomplicate the process. What works at your place? That's it.

Personally, I'm a fan of the new LED lights. I purchased a basic **Neewer Light Kit** on Amazon. You can purchase a set of two or three. I think mine ran me about $150. What I like about this set is they have rows of white LED lights and Amber LED lights. Both sets of rows are adjustable. Your goal is to adjust them so that **you pop from your background,** and you look like the right flesh tone for you. Not too dark and not washed out. If you can't afford a light kit, play around with a couple of adjustable gooseneck lamps. Experiment!

Many people choose to get ring lights. Hey, if that works for you, great. Personally, I'm not a fan because you can see the rings in your eyes or glasses. That can be a small distraction, but remember, you are the CEO of your home studio. Do some tests, get feedback and don't be afraid to send back equipment in the first 30 days if they don't work right for you.

As I've been upgrading my home studio, I often bought two different equipment options and tested them in my setting head-to-head. I then sent back what did not work. In front of you I suggest **two lights on either side of you facing in at 45-degree angles.** This way, unlike a ring light you are not looking directly into the light as you present.

I also recommend putting the lights higher than yourself, so any shadows are unseen behind you. Have a friend help you test and adjust so that you can be sitting in your seat as they adjust. If you record it, then you can both watch together later on to talk about it. Then test again. **Test again if you will be standing and remember the appropriate settings**. Once you get this right, you'll be able to just present!

One more technique to play with is a back light. If you get a third light, use that. If not, get another light that will go behind you. The purpose of this is to illuminate your background. It usually works best on the floor behind you pointing up at the background.

Your background should look professional and reflect your brand colors as well. I've seen many people, as I'm sure you have too, that they just never consider this. They look like they are in a cave, or you are trying to figure out what is behind them. That is a distraction that takes people away from your message and purpose. Make sure your backlight faces your background, not the camera! We should not see it; **we should see what it illuminates.**

Invest some time and get some help on your lighting. Once you get it set up, you never have to think about it again. **Lighting matters. It is your professional image.**

Darren LaCroix, CSP, WCPS, AS, Certified Virtual Presenter
www.BetterVIrtualPresentations.com Included with permission

Darren has done a series of YouTube videos on his virtual exploration. He was kind enough to allow us to share them at the resource page:
www.SuccessPublications.ca/PIVOT.html

Learning from Sesame Street (or newscasts)

Marc and I are members of CAPS, as well as founding members of Go Pro Speakers where Toastmasters learn the business of speaking. Marc Haine leverages design thinking as a Service Expert and Master of Experiences, working with organizations that need to build employee and customer loyalty. He is the author of **Lights! Camera! Action!** *Business Operational Excellence Through the Lens of Live Theatre.*

According to Wikipedia's *History of Sesame Street*, back in the late '60s, the creators of the Children's Television Workshop (CTW) realized that pre-school children were spending, on average, 27 hours per week watching a "wasteland" of programming. At the time, the content was based on entertaining children with what was deemed by CTW founders as "insufferably condescending."

Sesame Street was created as the first children's program that used research to design the look, the feel, and the content of the show, with a curriculum and clear, measurable outcomes.

Sesame Street was the very first show to test for attention retention. Segments were tested with children to see what content kept their attention and where that attention waned. Sesame Street was designed to teach capacity while maintaining the attention of their audience. Sound familiar?

Watch the nightly news on any channel, local, national, or international. I mean, really study them. Like Sesame Street, the broadcast is split into segments. Fast-moving graphics hit the forefront in the form of lower thirds–the bottom popups, announcing the topic or quote, and the speaker's name and position.

Animated logos and graphics announce that what you are watching is local, regional, national or world news. Segments are broken up with full screen flash ups with sound. The anchor desk and studio is bright, with active motions displays–some slow, some fast-throughout the staging. The anchorperson is shot from 3 different angles and lengths–close up (shoulders up), medium shot (mid-torso up), and standing, the full body shot. B-roll, secondary video footage, is played, with quick cuts (changing from one scene to another), as the reporter narrates over what the viewer is seeing.

Live, on-air interviews are done, switching from different interview windows (2, 3, 4 or more subjects) to a speaker-only window (full screen of one speaker). Anchors will punctuate a change in topic by looking at another camera, physically swivelling their chair to maintain body engagement.

As speakers, we need to learn from Sesame Street and the nightly news. It is no longer engaging enough to have a full-screen PowerPoint with the speaker in a thumbnail window for the duration of your presentation.

Look for ways to break up your content into segments. Finding points of engagement and different visual and auditory components changing every four minutes will keep your audience engaged. Smoothly switching from full-screen slides to windowed slides to the attendee's gallery view, especially during a discussion is helpful.

Definitely leverage polls, breakout rooms, and chats… but also encourage physicality on screen, such as getting the audience to hold up fingers, doing a shoulder-height thumbs-up, even dancing. Have them scribble their answer to a question on a piece of paper and hold it up.

And don't forget to use their names…. to this day I am still upset that my name was never called on Romper Room!

Incorporate games into your presentation. True/false Fact/Fiction… Where's Waldo, some form of Jeopardy or Trivia pursuit.

On stage you would never (I hope) stand in one spot, speaking in monotones. Programming your online presentation into segments helps the audience retain learning while creating a mental break from just consuming the information.

This chapter brought to you by the letter 'M' and the letter 'H.'

__Marc Haine,__ CFE, Certified Virtual Presenter, __www.MarcHaine.com__
Included with permission

Can you see me now?

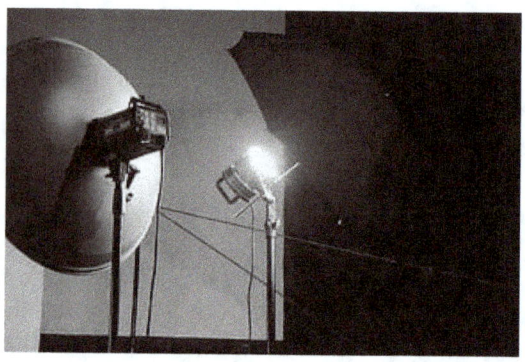

One aspect critical to presenting online is adequate lighting. That doesn't mean you need to invest in expensive studio lighting; it does mean you need to use it well. Make sure your face is well lit with one or two lights in that direction. I use two LED goose neck lights on either side of my monitor facing each other which provide good lighting for my face. In fact, they give me a nice healthy look. You can also look at adding something as a back light if using a screen to eliminate shadows.

Play with your lighting until you determine what helps people be able to **see you clearly** and be able to read your facial expressions in this new medium. We've added some great articles on lighting in our resource section on-line.

The Bitter Pill 'The Speaking Profession' Needs to Swallow

David is an amazing speaker and colleague and shared his honest reflections with us. David and I were to keynote the German Speakers Association event in Stuttgart this past September (2020). With Covid travel restrictions, David was able to pivot and present live from his home studio. I was able to pre-record my remarks which were shared with those who attended.

The reason why so many speakers have struggled to make the transition to effective and profitable "virtual" speaking is that they forgot **what made them great** (if they were great prior to the pandemic.)

When we got into the speaking business, we had an important message to deliver. We developed engaging content, our own speaking style and "voice." We worked hard on our stagecraft and presentation style to effectively communicate our message with power and wisdom, injecting humor and employing the art of the story. We had effective sales strategies that understood the business of speaking.

Then, as the proverbial rug was pulled out from under us by the pandemic, three very detrimental things happened to speakers — and they were largely self-inflicted:

First, we frantically scrambled to buy technology. We bought expensive lights, microphones and green screens. We bought technology a struggled to learn it only to find that our clients were using a different platform. Others made no changes at all.

We created webinars because that's what virtual meant right? We produced lots of slides and lots of words and maybe we appeared in the corner, if we even got it to work right. Others did nothing new at all.

What we too often forgot was that clients wanted our content and engagement and powerful delivery. With the distraction of technology, for too many, the content and the craft of speaking took a backseat.

Second, in a desperate attempt to ensure that our clients didn't forget about us, we rushed in to demonstrate value, and deliver value and offer value. Unfortunately for several months, it was all offered for free. Free webinars on surviving Covid 19, free webinars on staying positive during challenging times, free webinars on getting ready for the new, new normal.

And in our collective desperation to deliver value, we, in turn, "de-valued" our professions. We have trained the industry to ensure that our content is worth little, or at least far less. It may take years to recover what we have done to ourselves and re-establish fundable value in the eyes of the marketplace.

The last thing we did to ourselves was not only allowing ourselves to go off-track, but we also encouraged it. During the early days of the shutdown, there was a collective wringing of the hands by the meetings industry. Months of social media posts espousing the importance of self-care. "You should start journaling," said one speaker, to a chorus of affirmative comments. "Take time to walk in nature," said others, as dozens nodded in agreement. Misery loves company and there was no shortage of takers.

Meanwhile, we have mouths to feed and colleagues to fund and mortgages to pay. While hundreds of our colleagues were supporting each other emotionally, others were working day and night to **better understand the changing needs of our clients, creating captivating new content and alternative delivery models to produce and perform on a higher level — a level worthy of compensation.**

Seven months in (as of this writing) and it is staggering to see how many speakers still don't know how to share their screen or are looking down at their webcam or too close to the webcam, are backlit, or think it's fun to pretend they are on a tropical island with palm trees behind them on their green screen.

The world is forever changed and those who are biding their time and waiting for the world to change back are at risk of losing everything. Many of our colleagues already have. For our profession to recover and for speakers to once again be compensated for their brilliance, message, and solutions, we have to be more than merely participants on a web call. **We have to be Master of Communication once again — whether on stage, or on a webcam.**

David Avrin, CSP, Global Speaking Fellow, CVP
www.DavidAvrin.com Included with permission

A few reminders to effectively present on-line

1. Block out what you are going to say, just like you would for a live presentation. Great visuals, interactive, well paced.
2. Practice, so you are comfortable with your platform choice.
3. Tidy up your background so your audience isn't distracted.
4. Make sure they can see your face – adequate lighting.
5. Double check your connections and test your equipment.
6. Camera level with your face – some say eye level.
7. Minimize any potential distractions or interruptions.
8. Sticky notes: next to your webcam works great so you avoid looking down at your notes on camera.
9. Dress for the audience… no pjs or shorts please.
10. Make eye contact by looking directly into the camera. Imagine you are speaking to that one person, because you actually are speaking to individuals on-line.

Apply these simple tips to help ensure you present effectively and garner your best impact on-line.

Meeting tips for different types of virtual technology

We'll get to the more specific recommendations for each configuration of virtual meeting, such as phone calls, video, web, etc. Some of the previous tips will be repeated here from other speakers, consider them a reinforcement. Others are new and specific. Some tips suit more than one platform, and if so, we have put them in more than one list.

Tips for the phone meeting

Sit by yourself. Everybody should be connected the same way. A mix of some people sitting together and others by themselves makes for a worse meeting.

Be somewhere quiet. Don't sit at your desk where there are hundreds of things to distract you. Don't be at the train station, in the coffee lounge, the supermarket. Constructive listening is hard enough...

Use headsets that cover both ears. Good quality ones, too. It makes it that much easier to hear what people are saying and it makes it easier to focus.

Make sure you have enough battery life left. If you're using a cellphone or a wireless phone of some kind you need enough juice to last the whole meeting and preferably more, just to be safe.

Be on time. Good time. As a meeting leader it's good if you are the first one in the phone conference. A meeting leader should be ready five minutes before the actual meeting starts, just to make sure the technology is working and to greet everyone.

Don't speak too loudly among people. It's not at all necessary for everyone around you to hear what you're talking about. They probably don't want to and shouldn't hear it. Though it's preferable if you aren't around people at all.

Speak clearly. Any small amount of noise will make it difficult to understand. Articulate, emphasize and pause to make your message as understandable as possible.

Make room for breaks. If the meeting is of the longer kind, or if there will be natural changes of topic, you can have a smaller or longer break.

Eat and do your business before the meeting. You can't focus as well when you are hungry, thirsty, tired. Research has shown that judges tend to give harsher sentences before lunch than they do just after breakfast.

Be mentally present. How else could you possibly contribute to the meeting?

Slow down. In a phone meeting you can gain by reducing the tempo of the conversation to better understand.

Listen carefully. You can notice a lot more just by listening. Through both accentuation and silence, you can catch, for example, emotions and the speakers' opinion.

Write down the participants. That way it's easier to know who is always talking.

Mute yourself when not speaking. Turn off your input sound to lower the noise in the call. It helps everyone.

Don't fiddle with things that make noise. Even though it might not be very loud, it will still be heard. Keyring? Hole-punch? Coffee spoon and saucer?

Don't chew. Eating while in a meeting? It sets a bad example!
Tell everyone you're speaking. Say your name before you
start talking and nobody will be confused. This is especially
important when there are more than three people in your
meeting.

Try not to interrupt anyone. In a phone meeting it can be
hard but it's possible. If you must… if you do… apologize.

Take notes. Either yourself or through someone else you
appoint. You don't have to write down everything that is said
but it's good to at least get the decisions and tasks allocated on
paper.

**Every person that receives a task, repeats the task and the
time given for it.** This is best done at the end of the meeting
so that nothing vital is missed – no nasty repercussions.

Have good ways to start and finish. As a meeting leader you
can create good conditions by getting everyone going at the
start of a meeting and then finishing off nicely without stress.
Build relationships, summarise, and agree on who does what
next.

Tips for the video meeting

Sit by yourself. Everybody should be connected the same way.
A mix of some people sitting together and others by themselves
makes for a worse meeting.

Prepare carefully. Technology will sometimes just not work.
Far too many video meetings end with the group giving up and
switching to a phone meeting. It's boring and it drains your
energy. Testing everything with good time left before the
meeting starts will give you time to solve any problems that you
might come across.

Get closer. Don't sit too far from the camera; get closer (or zoom in). It makes for a better atmosphere and feeling.

Make room for breaks. If the meeting is of the longer kind, or if there naturally will be interruptions to change topic, you can have a smaller or longer break.

Eat and do your business before the meeting. You can't focus as well when you are hungry, thirsty, tired. Research has shown that judges tend to give harsher sentences before lunch than they do after breakfast.

Be mentally present. How else could you possibly contribute to the meeting?

Look at the camera when speaking. Don't look at your monitor. Precious eye contact is easy to lose compared to physical meetings. Less comfort, less trust, less creativity which makes it less comfortable.

Mute yourself when not speaking. Turn off your input sound to lower the noise in the call. It helps everyone.

Find ways to involve. Chat, voting, discussions, questions for randomly chosen people are a few ways.

Mix it up. Instead of just looking at each other's' faces you could maybe add a video or some pictures (relevant of course). This will break the monotony and make the participants more alert again.

Record the meeting. One advantage is that you can often record the video meeting so you can watch it later if there is something you need to check, and anyone not able to participate can watch the meeting afterwards.

Tips for the web meeting (webinar)

In a webinar there is usually one speaker, and the rest are listeners. It's comparable to a virtual theatre. In a web broadcast there can be audience in the same physical room as well as audience listening and watching through the Internet.

Be on time to go over the technology. The more technology the bigger the risk of something bad happening. Make sure everything works on your end.

Get closer. Don't sit too far from the camera; get closer (or zoom in). It makes for a better atmosphere and feeling.

Show slides if you have to. Sometimes it's harder to follow the presentation if the speaker is using slides that are not shown to the virtual audience.

Avoid long presentations. If it lasts more than 5-10 minutes, it can get tough to focus.

Let the chat be free. Give the participants the chance to reflect and ask questions in the chat function that is usually available.

Stop and interact with the audience. After each subject, after each big message, you should stop for a moment and answer questions as well as going through the chat to see if anything noteworthy has happened or been asked there. This will generate more energy and enthusiasm. It's not a bad idea to do this with "process slides" that don't have any information but rather some text like: Questions?

Pause. If the meeting is of the longer variety or if there are natural pauses in the meeting when changing subject, you can have a minor (or major) break to help people recover slightly.

Look at the camera when speaking. Don't look at your monitor. Precious eye contact specifically is something that's easy to lose compared to physical meetings which makes it less comfortable.

Use the shared "spaces" if you want people to create text or illustrations on a e.g. a virtual whiteboard.

Record the meeting. One advantage is that you can often record the video meeting so you can watch it later if there is something you need to check, and anyone not able to participate can watch the meeting afterwards.

excerpted Virtual Meetings by **Antoni Lacinai, CVP & Mike Darmell** *www.lacinai.se Included with permission*

I Lost My Voice

My creative friend **Robert Alan Black** *shared this story with me. When speaking virtually we are at the mercy of our equipment and internet. This could be filed away as a* **PLAN B** *in case something goes drastically wrong. Be creative!*

During the earlier years of my speaking career a few times I lost my voice. One time it happened with an annual client: Leadership Chattooga. I emailed the client I had worked with 5 or 6 years in a row that I was being called away and that I had found a substitute speaker.

He was a colleague named: **Dr. I. L. Create** and I sent her a 200 word or so biography to use to introduce him.

Then I spent Friday night and many hours on Saturday creating a completely **non-verbal presentation** using flipchart pads, posters for the wall, small packet of handouts. When she arrived at the training room at the University of Georgia Continuing Education Center the classroom was completely set up for a speaker. (*Could work virtually as well with PPT of Prezi*) 2 Flipcharts on stands in front of the room with welcome messages written on them.

Single flipcharts stand with blank pads at each of the 5 or 6 tables arranged for 5 participants. A single table in the front by the pull-down screen filled with many props.

In walked the 25 to 30 participants. As the time for the 3-hr session was reached, she stepped up front and read the introduction for **Dr. I. L. Create** and lead the applause as he (me in costume) entered the room to applause.

The entire 3 hour presentation was given without me SAYING ONE WORD. Yes, the various participants spoke at their tables and their chosen leaders did make short individual presentations of the results of their efforts The last slide on the screen and last sheets on the flipcharts in front all said thank and goodbye as Dr. I. L. Create left the room.

(Editor's note: brilliant idea to create both a memorable presentation and deal with a challenge in doing so. This could work virtually.)

Robert Alan Black, CSP <u>www.cre8ng.com</u> *Included with permission*

Foundations for Speaking Success!

When this material is taught in person, one of the areas covered as an overview is what I call my **'Foundations for Speaking Success!'** *Whether you are presenting on-line (virtually) or* LIVE... *these tips work. Just as you prepare before a sales call or client call in business, knowing in advance what you want to accomplish and how you intend to do it, is critical to your success.* **Reminder: This is doubly important in a virtual environment.**

Investing time to make sure you have completely thought through and answered these questions is essential to your confidence and success on the platform. These ideas were gleaned from conversations with fellow professional speakers across the globe. I've added to their wisdom from my own first-hand experience. These *'foundations'* have worked for me and **they will work for you!** The knowledge gleaned from their *wisdom* is the secret to being able to walk confidently up to the front and deliver a message that means something to your audiences.

The secret to ensure the audience gets the best presentation possible, with the most value, blended with personal stories and teaching points, **is in the pre-preparation**. This is what you do *well* before you start crafting your presentation.

Questions, thoughtful questions like these, can be the keys that unlock the door to success in any venture. This is no less true if your desire is to be a confident, powerful speaker, who connects with their audience, and leaves them wanting more.

WHY are you speaking?
WHAT do you want to accomplish?
WHO is your audience?
WHEN will you be speaking?
HOW long will you be speaking?
WHERE will you be speaking?

WHAT tools will you use?

WHY ARE YOU SPEAKING?

Major theme. What is it and why is it of importance to the audience? What is the central theme you wish to speak about? Why would it be of interest to an audience, especially this one? Is there a theme or major message your client would like you to deliver?

What moves YOU? What motivates you to want to speak about this specific topic?

Experience. Do you have some relevant experience that qualifies you to speak on this topic? What do you bring to the platform? How does your experience prepare you to share this message? How does it prepare you to understand their needs and build a bond with them?

Credibility. Why 'YOU' and not someone else? Do you have some academic, unique, or special job-related qualifications that lend support to you as a speaker? Have you done your homework in making sure you've fully researched and prepared for this presentation and this audience?

Background. How does your background prepare you to speak to this group? Are there shared or common elements in your background that give you a sense of what would be most helpful to those in your audience?

Answering these questions is a key to reinforcing your confidence and presentation skills. It will allow you to speak with greater conviction and passion. Make sure 'YOU' are the person who is well qualified and prepared for the presentation. Believe me, it helps!

WHAT DO YOU WANT TO ACCOMPLISH?

In April 1991, when I first joined Toastmasters, our manuals outlined various speaking projects that allowed us to focus on a specific goal in our speaking. Being able to know what end-result to shoot for helped me in preparing more effectively. Here are some of the speaking goals, as recalled, from the various manuals:

Speaking to inform? Do you have a new policy, procedure, or point of information to pass on to the audience? How do you make sure they understand and apply it?

Speaking to persuade? Do you have a passion for something and want them to change direction or follow you in making a change? Do you want them to buy from you, hire you, or promote you? How do you convince them you are the best person for the job?

Speaking to entertain? Is it your primary purpose to help them have an enjoyable time; to make them laugh and forget their troubles for a bit? This is a very tough way to speak, but if you do it well, you can enhance your career.

Speaking to inspire or motivate? Is your purpose to inspire them, to lift their spirits, to encourage them to try again or a little harder? What specifically would you like them to feel empowered to do when you are finished speaking?

Speaking with a call to action? Do you have a specific goal in mind that you'd like them to help you with? Do you want them to sign up, step up, or join you in taking a stand or an action?

Some other objective? What specifically is it you want them to get from your presentation?

Be clear about the end-results or goal in mind, while making your presentation is essential. Being able to pull the relevant information together will make your points come alive!

Be clear in what result you desire, what you want the audience to get from your presentation, or what action you want the audience to take.

As someone once said, *"If you don't know where you're going, any road will get you there!"*

WHO IS YOUR AUDIENCE?

Age ranges. Knowing their age ranges will be helpful in preparing and selecting stories, illustrations, and other supportive material. It will also help you determine how to structure your presentation for maximum effectiveness.

Gender Mix. Are you speaking to a group of men? A group of women? A mixed group? How many of each? Knowing this will help you present your message so it appeals effectively to both genders and ensures it will be understood in relation to their mind-set. It will also help you select examples or stories that are relevant.

Backgrounds. What do you know about these people? What do they do for a living? What educational background do they have? What ethnic or family backgrounds do they have? Do you have any common backgrounds, connections, or experiences with them that you can draw or build on?

Common bonds. Do they share any common experiences, bonds, or backgrounds? Are they all parents? Members of a special group? Volunteers? Do you have any connection with this common bond you can draw or build on?

Reason they are attending. Knowing why they are in the audience can be very important in your preparation. It is a foundation to making sure you present your message to maximize your chances of having them take it in.

Are they there because the topic is of interest to them or someone close to them? Are they there because they've been told to show up, by a boss or other authority figure? Is attendance a reward or punishment? **Makes a big difference!**

Knowing your audience is one of the essential keys in presenting a great speech. Knowing them allows you to present the information most helpful to them.

Doing your research and getting to know your audience can make a major difference. *Before undertaking any speaking engagement, I make it a point to talk in advance to some of the people who will be in the audience. This is even more important when you are speaking virtually.*

WHEN WILL YOU SPEAK?

Time of day. Make sure you know when in the day you'll be speaking. If you are speaking later in the afternoon or following a heavy meal, you will have a more difficult time with the audience. Early mornings can be difficult, too! If you are presenting virtually, you may be speaking in the middle of the night to connect with a global audience.

On the program. Are you speaking as a keynote or opening general session? Are you following 2-hour happy hours and a big meal? You're your remarks accordingly.

In relation to other speakers. Are you sandwiched between other speakers? Do you follow another speaker? Who are they? What will they be speaking on? Find out about your fellow speakers and their topics. Be prepared to adapt or change your presentation, stories, or jokes.

At one engagement, I was to follow Alberta's Lt. Governor **Lois Hole.** *The organizer asked that I be ready to adjust my time as Her Honour was known to occasionally go over.*

Lois Hole
1933-2005

I stood at the back of the room as she was piped in and watched in amazement as she stopped to hug people on her way in. Wow!

She was close to her time. I was happy to adjust my remarks following this wonderful lady, who was a credit to the Province of Alberta. I was asked to speak on her behalf years later when she was suffering from chemo and the death of her husband. Also, an honor.

Date and time. Make sure you know exactly when and what day you are speaking. Make sure you confirm it closer to the date. Seems a simple thing, but I know more than one professional speaker who missed an engagement when they neglected to confirm and showed up *'late'* due to a change. Don't schedule too close to the event start, either.

Early in my speaking career, pre-cell phones, I remember approaching our landing in Omaha, Nebraska barely 45 minutes before I was scheduled to speak; arriving at the hotel to find a very concerned client. Bad weather and a mechanical breakdown on two of my flights wiped out a 4-hour window and brought me close to missing my presentation. Now, I travel well in advance to make sure I am there; rested and ready to give my best.

Your time and position on the agenda can affect your audience's ability to respond or retain your message. You need to be aware of those factors and make changes to give yourself the best chance of effectively delivering your message and having it heard.

HOW LONG WILL YOU SPEAK?

Consider your audience. Have you ever been sitting on a hard chair, butt aching, eyes hurting, back straining while listening to a speaker drone on and on, oblivious to the time and the audience? Put yourself in their position and make sure you structure your time wisely for maximum interest and benefit for them. Focus on your audience!

Organize your presentation. Knowing how long you speak will allow you to organize your thoughts to make sure they flow logically. Also, if you have a shorter time period, you will need to get to the point quicker and support it with fewer relevant points.

If you are speaking longer, you'll need to **consider the following points in constructing your presentation.**

5-to-7 minute segments: consider the attention span of your audiences and try to design your presentation in smaller segments. People traditionally need a change of pace every 5-7 minutes, so schedule or structure your presentation accordingly. Wonder if this was why most of our Toastmasters projects were 5-7 minutes? Hmmm!

Group participation exercises. If you are planning a longer presentation, please incorporate some group work. This will allow you to take mini-breaks and allow your audiences to have a change of pace. You'll all appreciate it!

Consider audience involvement. Regardless of the length of your presentation, having audience participation is a key to making your message work. Ask questions? Get them to volunteer to help you demonstrate something, hand out something. Get them to briefly share with each other. Get them involved and keep them involved. More on this later.

Structure and time your presentation to maximize your impact takes planning and practice. The results are more than worth your effort!

WHERE WILL YOU SPEAK?

Location and logistics. Make sure you know precisely where you will be speaking; location, address, how to get there, and any other logistics that make it work for you to be there ready and prepared to do your best.

One speaker friend found himself checking into his hotel in the wrong town the night before he was to speak. Same name, different state. This made for a long night of travel to be there for the next day. I'll bet that from now on he double checks the location. This might not be a challenge in the age of COVID-19, but time of day and log in would be... see tips on setting up your speaking area for virtual engagements.

Updated: I remember laughing about his challenge. Years later, I had a client call me about an after-dinner presentation in Portland. I looked at my schedule and saw I was speaking in Boise, Idaho for two days in the early afternoons.

My thought, get a flight, fly over, deliver my speech, and fly back later in the evening or early the next morning. Or so, I thought! I told the client this and she laughed. She said, **"Bob, I am calling about speaking in Portland, Maine."** *I had thought she meant Portland, Oregon - oops! With the time change, I would have been late before I even left for the airport. I wasn't able to help her for that date, but she did hire me for the following year. (Now, being able to do it virtually, no problem. ☺)*

Room layout. How is the room laid out for your presentation? Give the organizer specific instructions if you need to set it up a special way for your presentation. Always get there at least 1-2 hours early in case it isn't set up. Sometimes, you will have to make do. **Don't be a *prima donna*.** You can always make some changes to make it work a bit better for you and your audience. This is your responsibility – use it wisely.

Sound system needs and capability. If you need one, is there one available? I'd suggest if you are speaking to any group larger than 40-50 people, it might be wise to have one. Make sure you arrive early enough to test it and know how to adjust it for comfort levels.

Audio-visual needs and location. What audio-visual tools are available for use? Do you need them? Discuss this in advance with your meeting planner or the organizer and plan accordingly. Always have a backup plan when 'Murphy's Law' strikes and the tool you were planning on using isn't available.

Hooey's corollary: Remember, 'You' are the message – bring it!

Climate control. Make sure you know where the climate controls are and how to adjust them or get help quickly. It is your responsibility to make sure your audience is comfortable.

You need to be aware of the logistics around where you are speaking. This allows you to prepare with confidence, by minimizing the *'little things'* that can worry you or detract you.

WHAT TOOLS WILL YOU USE?

Flip chart or white board. Is it visible to the audience? Use big letters, not too much on each page, and please use **colors** that your audience can see from anywhere in the room.

Keep in mind, you may have color blind audience members. Flip charts/white boards are great for smaller groups and interactive sessions.

Computer and LCD projector. Using PowerPoint or other presentation slide software can make or enhance your presentation. Make sure it is simple, not crowded, and not too slick. Hint: don't be too dependent on the tools. They are there to reinforce your message and they sometimes go down or don't work. Don't let them distract your audience.

TV and VCR. Do you have video clips? Please cue them in advance and make sure the equipment is set up and ready to go when you need it. Again, make sure you've assigned someone to help. Today most of this is shared with your computer and an LCD projector, but the guidelines still work.

What on-line platform are you using virtually? Make sure you are well acquainted with it and know how to use it effectively.

When I co-hosted the Cancun Wealth Creation Summit, we were fortunate to have a professional Canadian crew for our filming. I worked out the film clips and camera cues in advance with one of the crew members. Amazing how much professionalism it added to our overall sessions, and the follow up video series. Make sure your audience can see the big screen easily. **Hint: If it can't be seen, it shouldn't be used.**

Charts and posters. Keep them simple and make sure they are readable from anywhere in the room. Make sure they are sturdy and positioned for easy access.

Slide projector. Yes, this can still be a good tool, although your computer often takes its place today. Is it positioned correctly so everyone can see it? Make sure you've run through your entire presentation to make sure your slides are in the correct order and right side up. More so in the age of Covid.

Most of us use some form of presentation slides now days: PowerPoint, Keystone, etc.… make sure you have them set up so they are easily read and simple to understand. Remember they are they to reinforce or support you.

Handouts/learning guides. Make sure they are relevant to your topic. Give the audience a reason to take them home and use them or refer to them. Decide in advance **when** you will hand them out. If they are not needed during the presentation for reference, handing them out at the end of your presentation would be better. Let your audience know they are coming.

Props. Can be very effective tools in demonstrating a point or principle. Props work for keeping your audience involved in your presentation. Make sure they are positioned for easy access and are ready to go when you need them. Can everyone see them?

Costumes. Would dressing to illustrate your topic be a benefit? It might but consider it carefully. Make sure it enhances your message and credibility and doesn't become a distraction.

Selecting the proper tool to assist in making your presentation more powerful, more memorable, and more easily understood is an important element in your success. Always consider the size and layout of the room and the visibility of any tool you select. **If they can't see it, it won't work;** and quite likely will detract from your overall presentation.

Never use a tool unless you've *practiced* with it in advance. Make sure you are proficient in its use. If you fumble on stage, you will lose your credibility and possibly the audience's attention.

Always have a plan 'B': Murphy's Law was designed for speakers. Make sure you have back-ups and know when and how to use them. If something goes wrong, simply move ahead and switch to plan 'B' as smoothly as you can. **Be the professional in the room!**

Don't be dependent on your tools!

Having said that, speaking virtually, you are often very dependent... make sure you know what you are doing and have a back up plan if your internet or platform goes down.

Your audience is not there to *just* enjoy a slick multi-media presentation. They are there to hear you speak about something they hope will prove valuable in their lives and/or careers.

Choose your tools wisely; but don't be dependent on them. They are there to make you look good, reinforce, or support your points, visually demonstrate a point, or simply help keep your audience involved in your message.

Don't forget **'YOU are the message'** and these tools are yours to use to enhance your ability to get that message out effectively. Very much like the frames chosen to enhance a painting, your tools enhance and power up your message. The more *effective* speakers know how to leverage their tools wisely and professionally, so that the tools are not the focal point in their presentation. After all, **you want them to walk out of the room talking about you or your topic, not the visuals.**

Excerpted from **Speaking for Success**, *by* **Bob 'Idea Man' Hooey**, *Accredited Speaker, used with permission* www.ideaman.net

Kudos to Toastmasters International

When Covid-19 hit, Toastmasters International went virtual around the globe with clubs, Areas, Division, and Districts moving online for meetings and speech contests. We even had our international convention online this year. Our two premier speaking events, World Championship of Public Speaking and our Accredited Speaker level two were both conducted online.

This was a unique challenge for our speakers but ended up working well. **One of the benefits** of this is our ability to zoom into club meetings around the globe, and in some cases even joining clubs on a remote basis. We are learning to leverage our learning and our connections with fellow Toastmasters around the globe. www.Toastmasters.org to find a club near you.

Getting started presenting on-line

Paul is the immediate past President of the Global Speakers Federation. We have been friends and colleagues for quite a few years since he first invited me to come to PSA Netherlands to present at their 10th convention. We have shared stages, laughs, lessons and an occasional beverage around the globe.

When starting keep it simple. Start with some basics but in good quality. So, separate camera, microphone, and extra lights. You can buy this all for about $500: like a Logitech Webcam C925e; Trust USB microphone and a circle light.

When you start earning money with digital programs, then you can see how to use more cameras, different headlights etc.

Don't buy a green screen: use a natural background in your office or home. That looks more professional than the green screen standard backgrounds. If you want a digital background: go to Fiverr; for $50 you will have some very nice items to use.

Test how you are sitting: a lot of people, including professionals, are sitting in the dark, you can see their nostrils, or you only see their hair. Talk with family and friends and see how you are doing. What is the best way to use the camera?

Upgrade your Wi-Fi: check with www.fast.com how fast your WIFI actually is.
https://support.espeakers.com/portal/en/kb/articles/how-to-prepare-for-your-virtual-presenter-certification

Remote-software: zoom-pro is great; enough functionality for a good presentation. I use Webinar geek as well, for paid webinars: included are payment services, saves you a lot of time and money.

Check what you like best: sitting or standing; I see people walk around and then the sound is awful: you need to wear a mic on your body (Bluetooth)

Every 5 – 10 minutes creates interaction with your audience, whether it's professional or family. Keep them active.

Paul ter Wal, LLM, CSP Global, FPSA *www.paulterwal.com*
Included with permission

Studio tips

My NSA LV friends suggested touching base with Mark as he has created an amazing virtual studio and is producing professional events.

If you can afford to build out a nice studio, with built-in monitors, lighting, and a custom backdrop or wall. Do it!

I suggest using the green screen. You can go to a local fabric store and get bright green material for under $50.00 or paint a wall in the same color scheme.

If you can't afford a new fancy camera, I picked up a really nice cannon at the pawn store for $225- $250. There are many available on amazon that are even less expensive.

If that is too much, then invest in lighting. Use good lighting as that makes the less expensive cameras look great. There are some great lighting packages on amazon for under $150.00

With free broadcast systems like OBS you can really add a lot of effects and do some cool things to look like a pro.

Marvelous Mark, www.MMSpeaks.com Included with permission

Mastering your virtual meeting presence - Top 3 pro tips for upping your game

Greg Gazin is a long-time Toastmaster friend and leader. We have been sharing ideas and encouragement for many years. He is a professional writer (Troy Media) and blogger as well as a fellow member of Go Pro Speakers, a club focused on teaching Toastmasters the business of speaking.

Wearing a headset can reduce background noise and feedback

The right stage presence can make or break any performance regardless of whatever words may be coming out of your mouth. But as the COVID-19 pandemic has forced the world into lockdown moving our world on-line, many new "off-stage" rules apply, particularly in the widely accepted world of Zoom or maybe Microsoft Teams and the latest Google Meet.

An off-stage presence goes beyond a virtual stage presentation. It may take the form of an on-line meeting, a webinar, interview, recording a podcast, or just anything, anytime you're working from in front of a computer screen.

As humans we're not trained for the virtual world- but rather for a live audience. Professional speakers, facilitators, trainers and even Toastmasters, tend to train for a live stage. Managers may train to present in a boardroom while someone looking for work typically prepares for a face-to-face interview. So special considerations are needed when "presenting" on-line to take you from good to great.

The thought hit me about 15 months ago. I had just been on a somewhat disappointing webinar. Although the content was good, I pondered as a speaking professional, how much better the attendee experience could have been had the presenter been more cognizant that his audience was not before him but rather sitting in front of a screen, in the comfort of their own homes, possibly multi-tasking and likely faced with other distractions. *(The original ToastCaster podcast episode #113 from 2019.)*

I boiled it down to three major areas: **The audio, the video and you, the presenter.**

Think About Your Audio

For starters, think about the sound, not just the verbiage, what you'll be saying but about what people will be hearing. Know where your microphone is located what it's picking up and determine its sweet spot – the place where the sound is optional. Are you too close, too far, or too much off to the left or right? Are you speaking too loud or too soft?

Being too close or too loud may cause distortion. Volumes may be adjustable through hardware or software, but if it's overly distorted you may be out of luck. If you're too distant, you may be inaudible and upping the volume may simply boost the noise.

Find a quiet place to present. While street noise my not be totally unavoidable, you may be able to turn off ceiling fans or temporarily switch off your furnace or air conditioning and put your dog in the basement.

Using a headset rather than a built-in microphone and speakers, which can pick up stray sounds and reduce audio feedback, can reduce some noise. Rustling papers and the squeaky chair can also add to the distractions. And maybe turn away when sipping water of coffee.

Furthermore, when delivering, like a stage presentation, remember to ensure you introduce some vocal variety – the volume, the rate that you speak, the pitch or the tone, and don't forget the pause to let people absorb what you just said.

At first, this may seem unnatural in a sitting position, but doing so makes you more engaging, which is even more critical if you are presenting audio only with no visual.

In general, people may forgive bad video, but not bad audio. Think about that dreaded newscast you heard this morning

Ensure you know what the audience sees

Consider Your Video

The video, of course, is what people will be seeing. The viewer's experience depends on the lighting, what the camera sees and your positioning. If the light is too bright, let's say from direct sunlight or even a bright screen you will appear washed out. In dim light, you will appear dark, and the video will also appear grainy.

Test your lighting ahead of time – ideally at the same time of day you will be online. A naturally lit room is ideal but it's not always available. If you have the luxury of adjustable lighting, make sure it's in front of you. I find that having LED style lighting pointing at you at about a 45-degree angle works the best.

Like the microphone, know where the camera lens is. That's where you should be looking, not at your screen. Ideally it should be placed at eye-level right in front of you – you may need to raise your laptop with a phonebook or two like I do, otherwise it may appear you are looking down at your audience.

Also **consider your background**, what's behind you. Is it neat and tidy or rather distracting? Is your audience watching the TV you have on behind you or perish the thought you suffer the agony of Filipino journalist <u>Doris Bigornia </u>as her two cats broke into a fight during her live news show being broadcasted from her home.

Next, **think about your positioning**. How much of you do you want people to see? Personally, I like to be nicely centered in the window with the top of my head closer top, but not at the top. I also like, when possible, to leave a little viewing area to be able to see some of my gestures.

Body language can enhance your message and audience engagement

Watch Your Body Language

The third key to a great virtual presentation is Body Language – a balanced combination of facial expressions, gestures, and body movements.

People often forget to use their body language when sitting. That smile, frowns, rising of the eyelids and movement of the body. We all know that they too tell a story and add impact to your message.

When presenting virtually, people often go to the extremes. Some sit still like a statue, mouth poised on the mic and staring directly into the screen. Presenters on the other hand are trained to exaggerate gestures on stage in front of a large audience so they flutter about like the cartoon character, the Tasmanian devil, waving around their arms, swiveling, bouncing and rolling in their chairs. Often unbeknownst to them those movements are further amplified to a distracting level due to the proximity of the webcam.

You also want to watch your posture. How serious will someone take you if you're slouching?

Remember, body language is important even for audio only delivery. Can you hear a smile through the phone? Of course, you can. Even subtle inflections of your voice can act as an amplifier for your body. Try it. Be yourself. It will help you come across more genuine and natural.

Bonus Tip

And finally, here's a little **bonus tip**. Record yourself using Zoom. Their free plan that offers up to 40 minutes for a group presentation and unlimited time when you have two or less people including yourself on the call. You'll get both a video and an audio file that you can listen to and review.

Editor's note: You can even do it solo and still see and use your recording. I have done that when I am sending greetings around the world, like I did to our GSA convention in Stuttgart this past September.

Greg Gazin, DTM *Included with permission* www.outsmartthebutterflies.com *Greg Gazin, also known as the Gadget Guy and Gadget Greg, is a* **syndicated** *veteran tech columnist, communication, leadership and technology speaker, facilitator at Crestcom* **International***, blogger,* **podcaster** *and* **author***.*

In addition, Greg is the author of **Corey OutSMARTs the butterflies** *which is great for beginning speakers from 8 to 80. It is available on Amazon as well as* www.SuccessPublications.ca

Visit our on-line resources page:
www.SuccessPublications.ca/PIVOT.html

Judging perspectives

My friend Dilip and I met when we both spoke in the Accredited Speaker program in St. Louis, MO. He earned his that year and mine came in Palm Dessert a bit later. We have both been involved in judging and being chief judge for the live AS programs. This year Dilip had the challenge of being chief judge for the 1st ever Virtual Accredited Speaker program and assisting our judges in this new medium. In fact, the whole Toastmasters International convention went virtual with over 60,000 in attendance.

Here are some tips I have gathered about virtual presentations. Chances are that some of them have already been mentioned by other contributors. Yet, hearing these ideas expressed by different voices may give you insights on how best to articulate them. *(Editor: wisdom is attained from many perspectives)*

Speak to the eye

When presenting via your electronic device, make direct eye contact with the camera lens of the device, whether it be laptop, i-pad, smart phone, etc. When there are images on your screen, the temptation is to look at those images as if they are real faces. Imagine that the face you are talking to is directly on the camera lens of your device. Then, the listener will feel as if you are making direct eye contact!

Align the camera lens to be at the same level as your eyes

In order to do the above, you may have to raise or lower the laptop or other device you are using. I usually have a stack of books under my laptop to have it raised to my eye level. A webcam mounted above eye level will give the feeling to the listener that you are looking up at them. Vice versa, if the lens of the camera is below your eye level, the listener will feel that you are looking down at them.

Background basics

Set up your background so that it does not compete with you for the audience's attention. It's a bonus if your background supports the theme of your talk.

Attire

I like to wear solid colors when I'm presenting, as opposed to patterned shirts or jackets. The reason is that solid colors (a) do not compete with your face for attention, and (2) solid colors give an impression of authority more than patterns do. Of course, if you are giving a talk on a topic where stripes, polka dots, etc. will support what you are saying, that may be appropriate.

Importance of facial expressions and vocal variety

In virtual presentations where body movement and gestures are more limited than in in-person presentations, facial expressions and vocal variety gain added importance as a way to connect with the audience and convey meaning to your words. Variations in the rate of speech, volume, and pitch all give listening pleasure to your audience and engage them.

Gestures

At a live presentation, you can use a lot more gestures than in a virtual presentation. For a virtual presentation, use fewer, but well-planned gestures. Too many gestures may tire the audience.

Use gestures to pull in the audience

You can do this by extending your arm to the audience and then pulling it in to yourself. Of course, do this sparingly. See a great example of this in **Mike Carr's** winning speech at the 2020 *virtual* World Championship of Public Speaking - available on YouTube. *(Editor, it was creative and engaging and pulled us in.)*

Take advantage of the ability to make something appear very personal by putting your face very close to the camera lens.

But do this sparingly, otherwise it will irritate audience members. Several finalists at the 2020 World Championship of Public Speaking did this very well.

Add interest to what you are saying by occasionally using different angles to approach the camera lens.

This will contrast with always addressing the audience directly face-to-face. Do this sparingly. A great example is the way the 2020 World Champion of Public Speaking, **Mike Carr**, started his winning speech.

Pastor Dilip Abayasekara, DTM, PID, *Accredited Speaker*
www.drdilip.squarespace.com Included with permission

Kudos to our amazing teachers and parents who are helping educate the leaders of tomorrow

When Covid hit, schools were closed across the globe and students were sent home. Many teachers worked diligently to set up on-line to continue educating and supporting their students.

Parents were suddenly running home schools and grew to appreciate the work these teachers had done. Teachers also supported the parents in preparing lesson plans and augmenting by online learning. These are some of the real heroes in this on-going educational challenge.

Julie's gems…

Julie and I met when we were organizing a 2-day LIVE convention in Barcelona for this April. Sadly, we had to cancel and convert it to an on-line Speakers Roundtable. She is an amazing presenter and friend. Hopefully we will be able to host the event in 2021.

Have a great backdrop (not too busy that it distracts people!) I had one of my favourite mountain / lake pictures enlarged and printed on to a PVC hanging banner 2m x1.3 m. Everyone comments how solid and calming it is.

Set up lighting from the front with a ring light (you can also add side lights if needed) I use a 12-inch LUSWEIMI ring light which has several settings and works a treat!

Have your camera at eye level – not too close. Decide if you are going to be standing / seated / use a highchair and adapt camera & lighting accordingly.

Be the real you (virtually!)

Smile!

Choose clothes / colors that work well with the backdrop and a good fit for the audience you are speaking to (smart / casual / formal) I find plain colors are better than patterns.

Use your voice to capture everyone's attention and speak in bite size chunks.

Make it as interactive as possible – a dialogue versus a monologue – tell stories!

Make sure you are up to speed with the technology / platform you will be using and do a test run to check audio / screen share etc.

Invest in a good microphone – ideally roaming one if you intend to move around, Blue Yeti if stationary

Have fun! We are all adapting to virtual space, let's make it fun for all!

This is super basic – this is where I am right now. I set up the studio in my bedroom, eventually I plan to take over one room just for presentations / creative projects.

Julie Lewis, RAW, *www.julie-lewis.com* Included with permission

Always have a backup plan, or two

I learned this the hard way the other night in the middle of my **Go Pro Speakers** Advanced Toastmasters meeting. All of a sudden, my screen froze, and everyone did as well. I could hear the speaker, but no video. Then my screen went black. Panic! I eventually got it shut down and rebooted and waited.

During that time, I thought, why not power up my laptop, find the zoom invite, and rejoin quickly. My laptop decided it needed to update first… and so I waited and waited, some more. Then I waited until the host noticed me trying to get back in before I could rejoin. I had missed the last half of my friend's valuable presentation that I was to evaluate. Sigh.

Here is a simple solution. Consider the possibility of this challenge happening in advance and have another device connected to zoom or skype call from the beginning. A laptop, tablet, or even your phone. Call it backup. You can have the camera and audio off and simply turn them on if needed in the case of a disconnect. If sharing your message is important, make sure you are well connected to do so. Or have you phone set up as a hot spot to connect with the internet.

Ideas To 'Handle' Your Nervousness

Here are a few easily applied ideas and techniques on how to handle and overcome your nervousness: They apply equally to both live and virtual presentations. More so for virtual as there is extra concern and stress due to equipment, connection, and other tech challenges.

Don't fight it! Realize that being a *little* nervous is normal. I accept that and allow that nervous energy to propel me to a more impactful presentation. Remember, **"Nervous is Normal!"**

Being **mentally prepared** is a good part of winning and Speaking for Success. Being physically prepared is another aspect of the journey.

Do something **physical** to work out nervous energy. Take a brisk walk.

Don't sit with your legs or arms crossed as that impacts your circulation and oxygen making it to your brain.

Let your arms dangle at your sides while you're sitting waiting to speak. While your arms are dangling, twirl your wrists so your fingers shake loosely. Another way to reduce your stress levels.

Pretend you're wearing a heavy overcoat or jacket and feel it on your shoulders as your shrug them up and down to relax the stress in your shoulders. (We do that here in Canada.)

Waggle your jaw back and forth a few times to loosen it up. This relaxes your face and allows you to speak better and be heard.

Deep breathing can help, but don't hyperventilate.

Use the power of self-talk, say, 'Let's go!' or use some of the affirmations I share with you later in this Speaking for Success self-paced manual.

Don't be self-conscious about having a warm-up routine. Champion athletes do warm-ups because they know it helps them prepare to do their best. It also reduces the chance of injury. Warming up allows you to be at your best in front of an audience. It also allows you to loosen up and be more relaxed. Find out what works for you and build it into your preparation routine.

Here is a mental tip: Nervousness and *'being excited'* are two sides of the same equation. Mentally move into the *'being excited'* about the opportunity you have to share your ideas and to positively influence this audience's lives around the globe for the better!

Bob 'Idea Man' Hooey, excerpt from Speaking for Success! Used with permission www.ideaman.net www.successpublications.ca

Visit our resources page: We'll keep adding to it.
www.SuccessPublications.ca/PIVOT.html

Valda's suggestions

Valda is one of my Accredited Speaker colleagues who kindly shared her ideas. The AS is Toastmasters coveted professional level designation earned by 88 speakers around the globe (as of 2020). She is also an NSA board member who is an active leader in the speaking industry.

Make sure you know that your virtual background is a benefit and not a distraction. Test it out with a friend or do a test recording of yourself on Zoom.

Invest in a real green screen or make sure your makeshift one works (know what to do if you start to "ghost" - mainly just shut down and come back or drop the background and restart)

Test to see the right distance from your camera eye and practice speaking to the camera eye instead of looking at the person on the screen. It can be difficult, but it is a learned skill

Recognize that there is more fatigue associated with being online. Give adequate breaks and activities

Use tools like breakout rooms and polls judiciously. More is not always better.

Make it fun by asking attendees to bring something fun to talk about. An example is, when I talk about diversity I ask if attendees have anything, they have bought that helps them think of difference as a positive thing. They bring the object or if it's too big they talk about it and that serves as an icebreaker if one is needed

Whenever possible have a **"chat room monitor"**. It is so much easier to have someone pay attention to questions and field them or put them in groups.

Have a person who is paying attention to hands being raised or other indicators that a participant wants to speak.

Consider a virtual "producer" or assistant.

Pay attention to our environment regarding lighting at different times of day. My soft boxes make more of a difference at dusk than at mid day.

Have a back up in play before you start your meeting. Have a second computer (fully charged) where you have signed in as a co-host in case your main computer stops functioning. Same thing with a fully charged phone to use as backup. Know how to continue with a cell phone if needed (aligning with camera eye, no external microphone, etc.)

Make sure that the audio is good. You may be able to use the microphone associated with your computer or you may need an external microphone. Know it well before your event.

If you are using **"share screen"** make sure you can easily share and stop sharing. When you have PowerPoint or Keynote on full screen you may need to hit the escape key to get to a place that you can stop the share.

Determine if a webinar set-up is best or whether you want a fully interactive setup.

Of course, camera angle should be straight on and never looking up (like in your nostrils or under your chin)

Determine your settings regarding security ahead of time. Do you need to have a waiting room, password, require seeing/knowing the attendees to keep bad actors out?

Do you have the ability to add files to the chat?

Do you have the ability to let attendees share screens?

Can attendees unmute themselves or open their videos? What is best?

Valda Boyd Ford, MPH, MS, RN *Accredited Speaker, www.valdford.com Included with permission*

A few more tips...

Greg Wood is another of my Accredited Speaker colleagues from the Winnipeg, Manitoba area. We share ideas as colleagues and support each other. I had the privilege of being one of his judges when he successfully earned his AS.

One suggestion is to cross light the green screen behind you.

Make sure 'you' are well lit. 5600k is sunlight and is usually best. Have two lights out at 45 degrees

Have one light a little bit further back than the other to create subtle shadows in your face.

It is best to use a high-quality microphone as well. While we can get by with the built-in mic, the sound is so much better with a good mic. Your audience may forgive a poor-quality video but will not forgive poor audio.

Greg Wood, AS, Certified Virtual Presenter, www.gregwood.com Included with permission

"*One of the most important areas we can develop as professionals is competence in accessing and sharing knowledge.*"
Connie Malamed

Lessons learned presenting virtually

Joe is another Accredited Speaker colleague and friend who has pivoted to presenting online for Toastmasters Districts and clients around the globe.

Continue to be YOU. Be the same person virtually as you would on stage with one minor adjustment. Be 100% energetic because there will be no energy absorbed from the audience. Assume you are getting the desired reaction you are hoping for.

Practice using the virtual platform you will be presenting in. If you're using Zoom, set up your technical logistics so you can see and hear what you will look like when you present on the day. It's amazing what you will learn. For instance, during one of my practice sessions I realized I had to adjust my PowerPoint to make sure everyone could see the whole slide.

Seek help from those who know. Logistically I wanted to learn more about lighting, sound, and backdrop so I reached out to experts who generously supplied me with the knowledge I was seeking. I learned I needed to have white light in front and behind me and not to rely on sunlight because mother nature is unpredictable. I learned from Aaron Beverley, 2019 World Champion of Public Speaking, that the Yeti microphone is the most cost-effective device that will give you clear sound.

I have not regretted purchasing a Yeti microphone. I have learned the benefit of using a black, green, or white backdrop to ensure there is minimal distractions. Seek help from those who know.

Making eye contact is just as important virtually as it is on stage so:

Make sure your camera is eye level, so you don't appear to be looking down, or having it looking up your nose.

Make sure you look at your camera and avoid the natural attraction to look at audience members on your screen.

Stand or Sit? It really depends what type of presentation you are delivering and what type of presenter you are. I have presented sitting and standing. I prefer standing because I am an energetic speaker. Standing gives me that energy. I believe you can be as effective sitting or standing.

Joe Grondin, Accredited Speaker, www.JoeGrondin.com Included with permission

Virtual meetings and interviews

Over the past few years, I have had the privilege of speaking internationally on virtual summits, virtual meetings, and being interviewed by colleagues. This has expanded exponentially since Covid-19.

What a great way to continue sharing your ideas and connect with new audiences around the world. My guess is this will continue to expand as many organizations continue their LIVE events as Virtual ones, and more blended ones.

A few examples from this year:

Denise Marek's Calm Online:
https://youtu.be/RWSB3dBxNU4

Angelo Tihras' Future Summit – excerpt:
https://youtu.be/2E2YDDbd7U4

Think Differently with Marc Haine:
https://youtu.be/7IEgJxdHrx4

We also pivoted to do a 2.5-hour speakers roundtable in April to support PSA Spain with 16 speakers.

Tips for connecting better with your online audience

Kathy is a member of NSA Las Vegas chapter and I see her most Thursday nights for a Biz Accelerator zoom call. I find her comments and observations to be helpful each week.

The replacement for the direct connection is chat and questions using the platform.

You must get comfortable with the delay. For example: when you are speaking to an audience in person the audience can instantly raise their hand or simply interrupt audibly. Online when you ask a question, and you ask the audience to respond in writing there is a delay. Get used to giving them time to type their question or response to your question.

Leverage new tech to engage with your audience.

I love mentimeter. Why? I spend most of my time on gotowebinar. I am the only person on camera (other than my moderator who comes on camera occasionally). Gotowebinar has chat and questions as an option. We use chats for sending messages to the participants. We use questions which enables the audience to communicate with us directly. Only the participant and the moderator can view the individual questions/comments as they come in. What we miss in gotowebinar is the group interaction. Zoom enables this, but webinar platforms do not provide group interaction.

Mentimeter is an online collaboration tool. Attendees visit a webpage, enter in your code, and participate in giving feedback. As the presenter you can display the feedback and input from all participants on your screen. This brings the participants together. They get the benefit of other participant ideas and input.

Maintain eye contact.
Very simple and costs you almost nothing... **Put a post-it note with a smiley face just above your webcam.** The best way to engage your online audience is to make eye contact with the webcam. Leading online events is like flying an airplane. There's a lot to pay attention to. Having a simple post-it note on the webcam reminds you to make eye contact throughout the event.

If you are not competent with the online platform you are using practice, practice, practice or GET HELP.

Don't go it alone. Have help to manage the comments, questions, chats... You cannot do it all!!!! Your audience deserves your full attention. You cannot give them your full attention if you are attempting to read comments and chats, watch hand raising and other responses, and manage the application, etc.

My personal opinion: NO Zoom Virtual backgrounds!!!!!!
That is one person's opinion.

Kathi Kulesza, *www.kathispeaks.com* *Included with permission*

Retail pivot – great idea to connect and sell

A colleague of mine told me she was going over to a local high-end consignment store to try on a few things. The owner has been using Facebook Live as a venue to show and describe items she has in the store. She had seen a few she liked and asked the retailer to put them aside for her and set up an appointment to come in.

She ended up picking up a complete outfit for her next virtual presentation as well as a few extras. What a great pivot to keep in touch with clients and help them when we are all going through this challenge.

Humour and writing tips

Tom and I first met in Paris (May 2019) when we were keynoting the European Speakers Summit in Paris, France. He was amazing both as a speaker and in his use of comedy. We became friends and started sharing ideas. He was a value-added part of our Speakers Roundtable this April which was our pivot from a live 2-day event planned for Barcelona, Spain. Thanks for graciously sharing this material.

Why is humor so important in a speech? When people laugh, they are relaxed, and then they pay attention to the stage. Laughter has a connecting effect. People who laugh always look at their neighbor or partner, share the fun and check if the other person finds the anecdote or remark also funny.

That connection is a beautiful basis for a good speech. Of course, with a serious speech, you don't always have laughs on your hand. Even then, it is a good thing to put things into perspective now and then by making the group laugh a few times.

Ask yourself if the use of humor really suits you. Nothing is worse than someone who tries to be funny by force. That doesn't work. What's important is that you stand on stage full of self-confidence. Only when you are really credible, the audience will be relaxed enough to go with you when you make a joke.

During the preparation, you won't even think about making your audience laugh. After all, it's all about the message you want to pass on and the action your audience has to take. Still, it is helpful for yourself and the atmosphere in the audience if you let people relax with a funny remark when you come on stage.

If you can get your audience to laugh again after a serious story, the energy starts to flow back. It contributes to a good feeling that will stay with you after your presentation.

Why is laughing so important?

If you are going to investigate what happens when you laugh, you often end up with a biochemical explanation: lucky hormones are released, you feel better, it is good for your immune system, et cetera.

Still, it remains mysterious what causes a smile. I couldn't find any scientific reports on it, but I'll give you my view.

I think this is what it's like: from childhood on, you teach yourself everything from simple to complicated: fire is hot, water is wet, a child is small, bread comes from the baker, math is complicated. So, you have a hundred thousand logical facts, assumptions, and prejudices at your disposal. Someone who makes a joke plays with this. He starts a story (the set-up) according to a specific expectation pattern. As a listener, your brain doesn't have to make a lot of effort to follow it.

Everything sounds logical. But then there's a remark (the punch) that's completely different from what you've taught yourself. This is a total surprise for you. What's going on? The brain just doesn't understand it anymore. In a split second, you lock up and feel a kind of positive stress, which you then laugh off. After that, you relax again; you have a grip on the situation! So that smile arises to discharge the stress.

Pattern of expectations

I would have liked to give you a success formula for writing a joke, but unfortunately, there isn't one. After all, it's also about who tells the joke, where, why, and how. Those things can't be put in a formula. There are too many variables.

As a significant common factor, you could say that eliciting a laugh is the art of surprise. Like a magic trick. With his tricks, a magician plays with your expectations. He shows a box, shows that it is empty, but a little later, it turns out to contain a rabbit.

You're surprised: you can't do that, can you? Because you don't understand the situation for a moment, you are amazed, or you have to laugh.

It's not only about the trick but also about the overall picture. How is the magician dressed? How does he move, how is his timing? And is he standing in the theatre on a stage full of light, with rousing music, or in a dark corner of a bar? If everything on the show is right and he has a special act, then that's magical. If he is standing at a bus stop with the same act in his jeans, then the effect is significantly less.

Pretty tricky, making the audience laugh. As a serious speaker who makes a joke, you have a significant advantage: your audience doesn't see it coming right away.

The in-the-moment jokes

Some jokes arise spontaneously during your presentation and are therefore not conceived in advance: the in the moment or 'here-and-now jokes.' These often result in a much bigger smile than a joke you made up in advance. The audience feels that you are original. That witty remark, just at the right moment after someone says or does something, generates a lot of respect.

But these moments are scarce and cannot be planned. So which jokes can you think of in advance? Just by mentioning a few things you notice in the audience; you can get the laughs on your hand. On paper, there are no jokes in it, but at the moment on stage, it works well. It is often a matter of good observation. For example, you can name something from the hall or the location before you start: a crazy lamp, a striking mural, a lectern from 1948. Just something you notice. The more eccentric the example, the better. Or the duller, the better. It just depends on the twist you give it.

I was once in a room where dozens of old-fashioned cola bottles hung from the ceiling as lights. I opened with: "I was asked to give my perspective. I thought about it for a moment. Then I said, "If you hang sixty cola bottles in the room, I'll come."

This creates an excellent surprising effect on the people in the audience. Suddenly they all look very consciously at the cola bottles on the ceiling, which they had seen hanging on the ceiling before. Because of that connection, you have a perfect start for your presentation.

Preparing a joke

Jokes come in all shapes and sizes, of course. From one-liners to ingenious storylines, from bland to razor-sharp, from old to contemporary. A classic construction of a joke as we know it from the comedy scene in America and England is the 'set-up punch.' Now, this is not meant to make you a stand-up comedian, but you can take advantage of it.

Set-up

The set-up is the foundation of a joke, the original story you need to make your point. If the set-up isn't excellent or clear, there's a good chance the audience won't be able to follow you, even if the joke is that good.

The trick is to make everyone laugh at the same time. You must know what you want to say and whatnot. If you give too little information, you run the risk that not everyone can follow you.

If you give too much, you run the risk that your audience will be overwhelmed.

If you make everyone feel the same, you increase the chance that you can score with your joke considerably.

How could it not be? For example, it is better not to refer to a funny event in the boardroom in which only four people were present. You probably won't get a lot of laughs then. Nobody knows what happened there or what was said, even if it was so unique and ridiculous. In such a case, you'll have to tell the whole story to make the joke clear. Then consider whether the joke is that good; otherwise, it will be a moment like: 'You should have been there.'

Nowadays, you can watch performances of stand-up comedians on the internet via online streaming and on Netflix. Take a look at how a comedian does his set-up. You'll immediately notice how short the set-up is. It is quite possible that he directly takes you into his story in one or two sentences.

Set-up doesn't always have to be short; in fact, it can be amusing. Suppose you have a great joke about a garage. The set-up can already be strong by sketching the situation well. A young boy with pimples and a blank look. The mess along the walls that have probably been lying there for years, the 3D calendar from 2004 with half-naked women on it, the music in mono from a sound system with double cassette deck, with the quality of headphones that is extremely loud. This can certainly be a funny set-up, and you haven't even made the joke yet.

Keep in mind that it takes time to write such a set-up. A well-oiled story in which almost every sentence in itself causes a smile often seems to be a coincidence but make no mistake: it has been written and tweaked for a long time.

Obviously, your set-up has to be clear and straightforward. Your audience, on the other hand, can be totally different.

There are often kindred spirits in a business meeting: about the same age, the same background, the same work. So here, you will easily find a set-up that the whole group understands at once. With a diverse audience, it's different. If there are teenagers, vegans, adolescents, military personnel, parents, lawyers, anthroposophist's, fit fifties, yoga teachers, baby boomers, or a bunch of older people in the room, it is a lot harder to get everyone on the same page and take them into your story. Keep this in mind, whether it's a comedy show or a presentation.

Suppose you have a story that ends with a strong metaphor about Snapchat or Instagram, then you can score well in high school. If you come to a jubilee party with an average age of 71 where practically everyone still calls with a Bakelite phone, then that doesn't work. The same goes for the use of technical terms in your set-up. You have to be absolutely sure that your audience doesn't have to think for a second about what you mean. It seems like an open door, but I have seen too many failures to remember these warnings.

The 'punchline'

Your set-up has to be clear and only explainable in one way. The punchline, which follows your set-up and with which you make your point, must, of course, be just as sharp. Everyone in the audience should be totally surprised and see the image you present to them.

Your timing is critical. Make sure you end with the specific word that makes the whole thing so funny. If you still have to finish your sentence after the word that caused the laughter has already fallen, the audience will stop laughing because they want to keep listening. Gone is the effect. Of course, that's a shame.

So, the order in which you list things is essential.

Not only is the order of the joke, but also the structure and the information value of each sentence important. Look at this joke, which I have been telling on stage for years: *'I have a dog. It's a crossbreed between a pit bull and a Labrador. Strange character: he'll bite your leg off... but he'll bring it back.'*

It pays to think about the structure of your sentences. Don't give too much information and don't fill up too much time with unnecessary sentences. You can easily practice this yourself in everyday life. Are you at a party where someone starts telling you what he has just experienced? Then take a good look at what's happening. After two sentences, everyone is focused. It's a fascinating story, and in the end, everyone has to laugh. Then someone else joins in. In no time, the group of listeners is looking at each other from 'This is going nowhere.' Out of respect, they let him finish, and after an uncomfortable silence follows: "Who wants another drink?"

Watch out for situations like this when you're at a party or having a drink. Try to analyze why one says something that is entertaining and causes the other to kill the conversation. The chances are that both stories are similar. The first story is short and bright, with a beautiful plot. The second has far too much noise and wrong structure.

Write positively

It strikes me that people who start a conversation often use a complaining tone. It seems as if they intend to test if the other person experiences it the same way. Whether it's small talk in the schoolyard or at the coffee machine: they have to complain about it for a while. It is too hot, too wet, too crowded or too cold. They hope that the listener takes over their observation, and then you have a conversation about how cold it is.

It is fun to play with situations like this, to turn the conversation around and then see what happens and how the other person reacts. Cold? Perfect weather to test your mountain boots and a nice warm jacket. They work fine. Warm? Perfect for taking pictures of bees looking for pollen from the plants. The subject doesn't matter, as long as it's positive. The speaker comes out of his negative mode if you give the conversation a positive turn.

You can use this mechanism very well in your presentation. This way, you don't have to avoid negative things. Has a huge order just been lost? You can mourn about it, or blame a department, but you can also say: 'That's a perfect opportunity to put your heads together again and get back together as one team.' You decide how you deliver the message. This way, you can give a positive turn to every setback or negative event.

Write and speak visually

Whether it's a presentation, speech, theatre show, or story at a party: the trick is to tell your story visually. If your listeners can see in front of them what you mean, you not only have the perfect basis for a strong story but are also more likely to remember what you say.

Visual storytelling starts with visual writing. During the set-up, I already talked about the importance of being explicit and specific. That also applies to visual sentences. If you use a sentence in which the image is not concrete and accurate enough, it's a 'grey sentence.' It has no function. So not: 'There's stuff in a company hall,' but: 'The brand-new distribution center the size of a football pitch is loaded with product X. Everything is neatly stacked on pallets'—the more specific, the clearer the image. The moment the people in the room see the image clearly in front of them, they are captivated, and they are in your story.

You can make good use of the power of the image during the writing process to present your story convincingly. Build up your story based on images you see in front of you. Just like in a film, from scene to scene. Before you start writing, for example, try to see eight images in front of you, from left to right. An additional advantage of this is that you can also remember your story more easily during the presentation. If you lose your text for a moment, you can see the image in front of you and know where you are again. It also gives you a clear visualization of where you are working towards the last picture. This is where your 'plot' is the final goal of your presentation.

Be credible in your writing

A technique often used by professional speakers is the search for words. They really know what to say, but they do it to keep the audience up to date when attention decreases for a moment. If you, as a spectator, see a speaker thinking before he says something, then he will arouse your interest, and his speech will come across as credible. This isn't a 'rehearsed tune,' you think, 'this is coming from somewhere, this is about something.'

Obama was a master at this. When he holds his index finger in the air, looks away for a moment thoughtfully with a frowned-up look and then looks at you relaxed and starts: 'I believe...', then you as a listener are all ears.

A tip to come across as natural and credible as possible is that you don't write out all the sentences and then learn them by heart. Then the sharpness is gone because you focus too much on reproducing the literal sentences. A better technique is first to write out the story, and then choose one subject per sentence or block. When you read this word, you know what it is all about. The advantage of this technique is that you must rethink the sentence on the spot. Then it never sounds as if you are reading it or repeating it because you really must think for a moment. Not only does it look more believable, but it also sounds that way. What is important here is: learn from others but find your way to speak and never imitate anyone.

Exciting writing

Many comedians and cabaret artists start sentences like this:

Do you know what I hate?
Do you know what's outrageous?
There's one thing you need to know...

90

I had something bizarre the other day; it really happened...
Shall I tell you why I'm so upset?

They do that for a reason. They keep a show exciting, or they can involve a listener, whose attention has decreased, in the story again. There are two good reasons to use phrases like this in your presentation. **First of all**, a sentence like this raises a question in the mind of your listeners. They think: 'What do you hate?', or: 'What is outrageous?' and 'What should I know?', et cetera. That's what it's all about. With one sentence, you make sure the audience is open to your story. A second reason is that with a sentence like that, you adopt a personal attitude. You're touching on an emotion: it's now about an outspoken opinion.

In this way, your message comes across better, or the possible joke hits harder. After all, now it's not about just some information, now it's about what you think of it. Remember what I wrote in the introduction about the element's 'ethos', 'pathos,' and 'logos,' which the Greeks already used in their rhetoric. In this example, we are talking about pathos. Your story is emotionally charged with the above example sentences. And that creates tension.

Narrative writing: Storytelling

The business community has embraced storytelling. It's hype. But of course, storytelling is an ancient tradition. At a time when most people couldn't read or write, stories were handed down from mouth to mouth. There have been professional storytellers since ancient times. The fact that the concept of storytelling is now so trendy again is because these days we have a greater need for personal stories that touch us, as a compensation for all digital communication via social media and YouTube.

What exactly do we mean by storytelling? The most important characteristic is that you link a subject or product to a personal (success) story, causing your story to evoke emotion. We know that with emotion (pathos), we can influence the feeling and mood of our audience positively. The good feeling that listeners have after your presentation is automatically linked to the subject or product that you bring to the attention. Often, they remember it years later. That is why good stories are indispensable, also in business communication. Figures and specific details are less relevant nowadays because people in the audience can always look them up later. But you can't mail a 'positive feeling,' and you can't find it on the internet either.

This aspect is the success and added value of storytelling.

The advertising industry has long known that a message becomes more powerful with a good story behind it. If you think of Volvo, you see the European footballer Ibrahimović who links his personal success story to the success of the Swedish car brand. Heineken tells the story from 1889 about their participation in the Paris World's Fair, which they won.

You hardly see any shouting advertising of 'buy me,' but more and more often beautiful stories that seduce the viewer or listener, to which he can mirror himself. Tales of fifteen or twenty-five seconds that make you feel good, which you link back to the product. As a speaker, you can also apply this effectively.

Learning from beautiful stories

My kids love to watch Finding Nemo, Cars, and other animated films by Pixar. And I have to admit I like to watch with them, and every time I am surprised about how I am taken into the story as an adult. It doesn't matter if it's about a fish or a car. At Pixar, they have a good understanding of how to tell a story. This is evident from their turnover, which exceeds eight billion dollars a year.

I went to analyze how such a story is constructed, just to see if there was a general formula or a fixed pattern behind it. I came to the following: the story starts with the main character in a (for him) everyday situation. Then something remarkable happens (often a disaster or a drama) with all kinds of consequences that need to be solved, and it ends with an excellent positive plot, usually involving a bit of morality. This was my 'gut feeling' about the construction of the story in their films.

After some research, I found an article by Emma Coats. She has worked on many Pixar movies. She once kept track of Twitter of the process of the creation of such a film. In one of the tweets, she told me exactly what I had come up with. Six sentences.

Once upon a time...
Every day...
One day... (something remarkable, strange, awful)
Then problems had to be solved...
Then it happened...
Until..., look where we are now!

So, Pixar - and no doubt any other good filmmaker or writer - use this starting point to tell an exciting story. It's as simple as that! You can use this too. It offers you a guide to building your own story. If you don't have anything on paper yet and you follow these sentences, then suddenly there's... a story.

Using figures of speech

What can we all use to write a good story? As you've read by now, I like to look at examples from other disciplines, such as advertising or movies. From literature, we can not only learn something about the construction of a good story - as explained above - but also about the figure of speech. With the right figure of speech, you can make sure that you give color to your story, that it becomes lively. You can use it to take the tension away from a message that is difficult to tell or to emphasize what you stand for. Finally, you can use figures of speech to bring humor into your speech.

Metaphor

The word metaphor comes from the Greek and literally means transmission. It is a form of imagery that involves an implicit (unspoken) comparison. With a metaphor, you can describe expressively a situation that runs parallel to what you want to say.

So, you can mirror your own story in a metaphor. The greatest strength of this is that you disconnect your existing story from reality, as it were, and with the metaphor, you have more freedom to make something clear. This means that you don't name a particular person or company, but something that resembles it. This allows you to be more provocative, to go close to the edges more. And because the metaphor is a story in itself, the audience will also remember it better.

But how do you find a good metaphor? When you hear a metaphor, they always sound logical and seem to be easy to come up with. Still, it's a bit of a search. You will have to sketch a number of situations that you can mirror to your story, and then figure out which one fits best. How do you do that? Search your own story (or part of it) for the characteristics of the layer beneath it. What exactly do you want to tell?

What is the message? What is the problem? What is the meaning of your story? What do you want to make clear? Are you angry, delighted, happy, excited? Search for a familiar situation with as many characteristics as possible that match your story. Make sure that it is a situation that all people in the audience immediately recognize it is not the intention that you have to explain a metaphor. If all goes well, the pieces of the puzzle will immediately fall into place.

Exaggeration

Children love to exaggerate. You might wonder who taught them that. It is, therefore, no surprise that many adults exaggerate in their daily communication. It seems that men tend to overestimate more often about facts, figures, speed, and size and women about emotions and feelings. You can be bothered by exaggeration, but it's also part of it. In fact, we are so used to it that we don't take everything someone says literally. Think of common sentences like: 'She scared the shit out of me' or 'If she says that one more time, I'll never have to see her again.' And how about, "I'd kill for a cup of coffee.

Precisely because everyone in daily communication is used to the fact that not everything has to be exactly right, as a comedian you have to put exaggeration in your story - if you use it as a stylistic tool - go all the way. Otherwise, it won't even stand out anymore.

A few examples of sentences that don't even stand out anymore:

"Where were you? I've been waiting for you for a century...
"That's the hundredth time already.
The classic: "You were the best audience I've had in ages.

Below are a few examples of strongly exaggerated exaggerations:

"We're not going to import the products from Korea. The delivery times are extremely long; that will only make sense if my grandchildren inherit the shop later, and we also want to sell retro stuff by then'. (By the way, this isn't even such a bad idea, as long as you have a storage space where you can store your stuff for forty years, free of charge and safe).

'Turnover has doubled every time in the last two years. From two percent to four percent market share, and this year to eight percent. If this continues, in four years' time, we'll have a hundred and twenty-eight percent market share... Cheers! '

Understatement

An understatement is a deliberate weakening. You say something in a way that seems so much milder and cooler than you mean, that the evoked contrast produces a comic effect.

A few good examples:

"So, you've only achieved twenty percent of your target. Well, um... That's not bad. I hope your next employer's doing better. We've fallen from an 8.7 to a 3 with customer satisfaction. I think some things didn't go quite right.'

Irony

The definition of irony is 'feigned ignorance.' You make something clear by saying the opposite of what you mean so that the remark comes across as milder. Irony works better in speech than on paper. After all, you can use body language or the use of your voice to indicate that you mean the opposite with your remark. Moreover, if you notice that your remark is wrong, you can put it into perspective or reinforce it. It is up to the reader to find this out for themselves on paper.

What the effect of an ironic remark will be is, of course, also up to the speaker. If you have always been ironic, the audience will expect it sooner, and it will suit you as well. Someone who is always cheerful and positive should make more effort to come across as ironic.

A few successful examples:

'And then they closed that bridge here for another two months. Fortunately, that didn't matter at all to our logistics department.'

'We must work really hard to communicate with each other, also between the different departments. But what I find hopeful: when I look into a room like that, I see that almost all noses are in the same direction. Only the sales department looks at the entrance on the right. But that's probably to see if any new customers are coming in.'

Irony can well be applied to name certain, less pleasant circumstances in the room at the beginning of your presentation. Suppose you are standing in front of a half-full room with an empty first row. If you want to start sharply and are allowed to provoke a little, then open up with: 'Fine, an empty row like that, I immediately feel the love from the audience... 'Often people sit in the second row because they don't want to get questions. You can play with that by saying: 'I see now that the second row... becomes the first row.' By naming the situation, you indicate that it does not bother you.

Self-mockery

With self-mockery, you make fun of yourself. It is a strong weapon for an artist. The audience loves it when someone dares to admit their weaknesses. You can also use self-mockery as a defense mechanism: if you immediately acknowledge that you have done something wrong, you can no longer be judged. You also take some of the tension away from the audience by naming what they might think.

Still, self-mockery must come from certainty. You name a personal deviation from yourself, but you must be strong in that. It shouldn't become pathetic or come across as if you want compliments or are looking for comfort. Then it becomes uncomfortable. Suppose you have a scar on your face that immediately catches the eye. Then it is strong if you have a good story about it. Then you may seem vulnerable, but still, you radiate that you dare to tell this here.

Play on words

Few stage performers use the pun as a figure of speech. If they do it at all, it is often a guilty pleasure, to use an English term again. You can play a pun in such a way that you show that you can't actually do it, but that you do it anyway. Then the challenge is to come up with a powerful one. Often you see word jokes coming in advance, or they are not strong enough. Just one example: 'It's a pity that the exporter doesn't do anything.

Call back

A call back is a repetition of a remark or situation that you have mentioned before. This is essential for any message you want to convey. The word advertising comes from the Latin word 'reclamare' and means repeating your message.

In addition to your message as a callback, you can also use this technique as a figure of speech to get the smiles on your hand. It is a technique often used in theatre: you make a joke about a certain situation or person, and a while later, you let exactly that situation or person come back in your story. The great thing is that the audience - if they have laughed the first time - will have a full laugh again the second time. Usually, there is respect for a callback, and the audience thinks it's clever that you're thinking about it.

How do you use a callback? For example, at the beginning of the speech: 'Over the past two years we've been aiming for 4% growth, but despite the turmoil in the market, I think we should aim for 8%. Then, after a quarter of an hour: 'I recently heard from a great economist, really a man with a vision that you have to strive for 8% growth in our industry'. And then finish with: "Okay, 8%. Deal! Thank you for your attention.
What catches on is a call back from the interaction. Suppose you have an interaction with someone in the audience at the beginning of your speech. You find out that this person is a

marketing man and that his name is Rob. Later, in your story, you talk about a marketing man. You say that these people are so shrewd and always think three steps ahead. And then you say: 'Rob knows exactly what I'm talking about.' With this, you give the audience the feeling that you're not writing a standard story, but that you're really involved with them. You're in the here and now. You can also think right in advance that you're going to make a callback. Then watch the audience before you stand up and find someone you can use for this.

This way of preparation does require some improvisation; after all, you never know correctly whether this person will react in the way you have in mind.

Stock lines

Imagine giving a presentation, and after ten minutes, someone from row five gets up and walks out. That always creates a certain tension. The most important thing is that you mention that as a speaker right away. The chances are that the audience will find it uncomfortable. 'Why does someone leave? Isn't it interesting?'

The moment you mention it, that tension is gone. Of course, you can be surprised that someone just walks away. Either someone shouts something out of the room, or a tray with glasses falls. Then you can use the so-called stock lines. Stock lines are sentences that you can use - if necessary - immediately to counter an event, without thinking about it. Stock means stock: these sentences are ready to be used on a 'shelf' in your memory.

Stock lines are used if you lose control during your story. This loss of control can have all kinds of causes. Sometimes it's up to you as a speaker, you've said something that doesn't catch on, or is downright stupid. Or you don't know what to say anymore. The tension that then arises in the audience, you take away with a stock line. You press the reset button, as it were.

99

You can sometimes end up on stage in a situation where the loss of control is not your fault. Suppose someone in the audience shouts something crazy (at the English comedy shows they call it 'to heckle'). Everyone turns to the person in question and then to you. What do you do then? Then it's better to name those circumstances and say something about them than just go ahead and pretend nothing is wrong. Use a stock line to silence that person.

In general, the public is good. It is not customary to deliberately make things difficult for someone on stage. What can happen, however, is that someone from the audience spontaneously says something hilarious, causing the whole audience to laugh. Of course, you just must let this happen. In fact, give him the credits he deserves.

You have the microphone as the speaker, so you can always take the word back. I came across a nice heckle on a comedy forum, now a classic: the singer Bono is at a big festival in Glasgow. After a certain song, he stops the show, walks forward, and slowly starts clapping his hands, saying: 'Every time I clap my hands, a child dies in Africa.' Someone in the audience is shouting, 'Stop f**king clapping then!'

How Bono got out of here doesn't tell the story, but I hope for him he had a brilliant stock line on the shelf.

Or how about this one:
A comedian on stage says, *'I'm a schizophrenic.'*
Someone in the audience: *'Why don't you both take off?'*

It won't be easy to get a heckle during a serious event, but it's still useful to know that they exist. By using a stock line, you keep the last word, and you avoid giving the impression that you don't know anymore.

If you don't have experience with stock lines, the following example sentences might help. Put them on your mental shelf, who knows; they might come in handy someday.

Suppose you start your story, but a group of people from the audience just keeps talking. It bothers you and the rest of the audience. Then you speak to the group: 'Sorry I'm talking through you all the time. It's also crazy; you're chatting in a room, suddenly someone starts a presentation... You don't expect that, do you?' ☺ .

Another example: if someone shouts something meaningless through your show, you can recall: 'You shouldn't drink on an empty head.'

At the end of your presentation: 'They say you have to stop at the climax. That was about twenty-three minutes ago. The number of minutes can, of course, be replaced by another timestamp: 'That was about three years ago....'

When people run away during your performance, you say, 'That's right, I'd rather you leave.' Say it with a broad grin, because it may be that someone has an important reason to get up and leave the room. Yet it is a confrontational situation that not only affects you as a speaker, but also the audience. Through such a stock line, where you name the circumstances, you show that you do not allow yourself to be upset. And if you say it with a smile on your face, you take away the tension that has arisen in the audience. Especially with the addition (to the audience): 'Well, I'll get larger halls empty.'

How do you get good stock lines? Of course, it's not done to use a sentence from another comedian. But at the same time, that's the tricky thing about many stock lines: nobody knows where they come from or who came up with them. In general, a stock line that has already been used by several speakers can be considered public, and can, therefore, be placed on your own 'shelf.' Be careful with stock lines. Think of them as parachutes.

It emerges in emergencies. A stock line does that when you crash on stage.

If you often stand in front of a group, there's a good chance you've already created a stock line on the spot a few times. Try to find out what kind of sentence that was. It's always better to use your own stock line in an awkward situation - after all, it suits you better.

Misleading the public

You can catch the attention of the people in the audience well by misleading them with a remark. That way, you play with their expectations. These kinds of comments are not meant as a razor-sharp joke, but they can sometimes offer just a bit of relaxation in a serious story. You show that you like to play with the audience for a while. An example: 'What Jos has done for the department is unbelievable, thank you for that. If anyone would earn the cup for 'best employee,' it would be Pete. Because he had to work with Jos all year long. Pete, a great guy.'

Or: 'It is now almost half-past six, the end of a long day and a fantastic meeting. I would like to thank the organizing committee for this day. Without them,' here you wait for the effect, 'we've been drinking beer in the sun for three hours now.'

Pay attention to how you present an image in the first sentence that is completely clear. The sequel shows something completely different from what your audience has in mind. This game with expectations makes people laugh. It's just liked the set-up and the punchline I dealt with earlier.

Tom Sligting, *Director Personal Disruption,*
www.nextglobalspeaker.com *Included with permission*

Using Humor... A Few Safety Tips

Humor doesn't always travel well and can be mis-understood depending on who is in the audience. **If in doubt, leave it out.** *Check with folks who will be in your audience to see if what you have planned works. More so now when speaking virtually and your audience is global.*

In the professional speakers' world there is a saying in response to the question, **"Do you have to be funny? Only, if you want to be paid!"**

While that is not entirely true, humor, when properly used, does make your presentation more interesting and helps build bridges with your audience, whether live or in a virtual setting.

Here are a few tips to remember if you plan on including *relevant* humor:

Punch lines? Remember them!!!! Practice until you can nail it if awoken from a dead sleep.

Ensure the anecdote is appropriate and relates to your presentation – not just inserted for the laughs. Too many amateurs undermine their efforts when they insert something fun that doesn't relate to their audiences.

Timing is everything – practice it! A lot!!!

BE KIND! Don't pick on any group or person. Pick on yourself! This also helps build bridges with your audience by showing you are a real, authentic person.

Vulgarity and sexist remarks are NOT allowed. They always work against you.

Humor doesn't travel well. Make sure it works in different locations. Humor doesn't always translate to other cultures.

And please, be aware of any physical gestures that might be offensive in other cultures as well.

While speaking in Tehran, Iran (2009) I shared a story that always got a laugh in North America.

Nothing! Dead silence! No laughter, no chuckles, nothing!

I asked the translator about it and he said, "I didn't get it!"

Once I explained it to him, he laughed and said, "That's funny!"

Later that week we used it again in Kish to 300 international university students, and we got laughs, lots of laughs. He was funny and he helped me bridge the cultural laughter wall.

Lesson learned: Discuss any critical or humorous pieces with your translator to ensure nothing gets lost in translation.

Bob signing books in Tehran, Iran

Bob Hooey, *CVP, AS, Spirit of CAPS Recipient, Excerpt from Speaking for Success Used with permission.* www.successpublications.ca

"Think twice before you speak, because your words and influence will plant the seed of either success or failure in the mind of another."
Napoleon Hill

A few tips from Terry

Terry and I know each other from Toastmasters. We each earned our coveted professional level Accredited Speaker designation. We even had our AS level two judging this year virtually. So, we have our first virtual Accredited Speaker in our TMs history.

In Zoom meetings attention spans are less than in person. **We need to get to our point more quickly.** No long slow build ups. Get to each point. Still use your stories to illustrate points, but we need to get and keep the Zoomers' attention immediately and keep it throughout the presentation.

PowerPoint has for the most part been poorly used even before Zoom. Very few have taken the time to learn what makes a good and bad PowerPoint presentation. Take the time to learn how to use it and how to make it powerful. With Zoom it is even more critical they can see and benefit from what you display because it will be most of their screen. Simple rules such as no more than 6 words per line, and no more than 6 lines per slide should be used. The same with pictures or graphs.

Make them simple. Make them large.

Don't crowd your slides. Better to have 20 slides that show one line at a time than 1-2 slides with so much people get confused.

Don't show all bullet points at once. Use animation to have them appear as you begin to talk about each point.

Don't get caught up with fancy entrances or transitions for pictures or text. Keep it simple and consistent.

Be professional. Let everyone else wear t-shirts. You don't need a suit, but at least a collared, buttoned shirt. Something equal for women.

Manage your background. People want to see and hear you, not your cluttered desk, or bookshelf, or you fading in and out of a green screen of you in outer space (yes, I actually saw that on a professional presentation).

Go on Zoom by yourself and see what you will look like, and most importantly what your attendees will see. (Practice!)

LOOK AT THE CAMERA! They will be looking at you. You are looking at notes, your keyboard, others on the Zoom will not show them that you are talking to them. Look at the camera. If you need notes have them placed next to the camera and out of view so you don't have to look down or to the side to see them. **Keep them VERY simple.**

Stand up. Attendees don't need to see all of you, only from about mid-waist ad up. There should only be minimal space above your head. Make yourself as large as you can without cutting any of you off. Even if they only see your face stand up. It will give you more energy and enthusiasm which will help keep their attention.

If you are not the host, make sure the host has you as a co-host or assigns you as the host when you present. Have your PowerPoint cued and ready to share. You don't want to take time looking for files or setting up. Do all you can before you go on.

And, as always with in person presentations, smile! A smile on your face calms people, lets them know you are enjoying what you are doing and helps them enjoy it, too.

May all your Zooms be memorable (for the right reasons).

Terry Mayfield, AS, www.terrymayfield.com Included with permission

[Renaming game]

Jackie and I became friends when we both spoke at an event in Cape Town, South Africa many years ago. She has been ahead of the curve in leveraging online training and was kind enough to share these ideas.

I'm renowned for devising creative icebreakers, energisers, and games to enliven on-site presentations. Now, I do that for online presentations too.

We've all heard of "Zoom fatigue".

Online, I believe you need to set the audience an activity at least every 15 minutes to keep them engaged.

Like so many others, I've had to switch my full-day training sessions to Zoom. The advantage is that no-one needs to travel, and attendees can join from anywhere in the world.

Once, there was a participant from Australia. As I'm in the UK, I had to think really hard about what I could do to help keep her attention until 2am Melbourne time.

Here's one idea that you might find useful.

During the introduction, get people to rename themselves to include the number of years' experience they have.

Then later, when you let Zoom sort them automatically into breakout rooms, you can ensure there's a nice mix of experience in each room, and manually 'move' anyone if you need to.

People can also see each other's experience while in the main meeting and in the rooms, so they know who to take seriously.

I suspect it also subtly encourages the more senior attendees to speak up and take the facilitation role in each room, without you needing to contrive that.

It's also useful for people whose **device is called 'iPad2' or similar, because it gives them the chance to edit it to their real name without you having to request that.**

It works because they see there's a *point* to doing it. It's not just a random icebreaker activity.

Note: only desktop and laptop users can rename themselves while in a Zoom meeting. Tablet and phone users can only do it before they join.

To overcome this, you could **start the meeting with a standard poll asking what device people are using,** so you can give relevant instructions. If there are any tablet/phone users, invite them to message you in chat (publicly or privately) with their number of years' experience. As host or co-host, you can then discreetly rename them.

To rename yourself (or other people if you're host or go-host), open the participant panel and hover over each camera icon. 'Rename' will appear as a drop-down option.

Note: renaming only lasts for the duration of the meeting. Next time you open Zoom, it will default to your usual profile name.

The first time I tried this was effective and helped create a lovely energy. At the end, I invited the group (24 attendees) to exchange contact details in the chat so they could stay connected afterwards and continue to support each other if they wanted. They were keen to do it.

I was delighted with how the meeting went. Even those with cameras firmly off at the start ended up with cameras on, and there was lots of laughter throughout. During my training days, we do lots of other interactive things too, of course.

For loads more ideas about audience engagement, online and offline, please see https://experientialspeaking.co.uk/

Jackie Barrie, *Certified Virtual Presenter www.jackiebarrie.com*

Guides for giving an effective virtual presentation

1. **Be brief:** audience attention is less than in person. I have heard less than 10 mins, so be brief and to the point.
2. **Keep it simple** with slides and graphics.
3. **Act like you are on TV**, looking and talking to the camera.
4. **Be doubly prepared** and familiar with your tools.
5. **Get assistance** – have someone helping with the techie stuff and with monitoring chats etc. Focus on your talk.
6. **Be specific** in asking pointed questions to avoid chatter.
7. **Log on early** and encourage your audience to do so too. This allows you to build rapport before you present.

My Journey to Running Online Summits

You may not want to leverage your virtual message in this ambitious adventure, but you could. I had the privilege of being one of Angelo's speakers on The Future of The Future Summit, speaking on the **Future of Business.** *He worked hard behind the scenes to make sure it flowed and keep all of his attendees engaged. He made it look easy, even when, I know from experience, it wasn't. He was scrambling to pull it together behind the scenes. Sometimes you do your homework as you grow.*

If you had told me a few months ago that I would be where I am today, I would have laughed in disbelief. And yet, it is what it is.

Everything started off as an idea and getting 2-3 random "signs" of confirmation.

The first was checking if the domain name was available, it was. Next was the cost, which was only $8. The next was bouncing the idea off someone I trust and admire. For the first time in a long time, they went silent and eventually said, "I have one thing to say, DO NOT screw this up! You're on to a winner here!".

This subconscious process was applied to every element of the summit creation:

Discover what needs to be done

Learn it how to do it

Do it

Repeat

Ignorance is your friend, complacency is not. This is one element that I would recommend to anyone starting such an endeavor, especially if they are doing it alone. The more you are aware of what needs to be done the overwhelm might stop you from starting at all. However, if you do start, make sure you give it your 100% and more in every aspect. It will be worth it.

I was also on a budget so there were many "hacks" that needed to be done.

Some of these 'hacks' are:

Using a mobile phone and $10app (epocCam) as a webcam instead of buying a $200 webcam.

Second-hand lighting bought online.

$15 lapel microphone instead of an expensive desktop mic.

Designing my own website on wix.com instead of getting a pro to do it.

Paying monthly instead of yearly for my platform (Kartra). This is a short-term saving but long-term expense as a yearly subscription would be cheaper if calculated monthly.

Using "Google Suite" ($8/month) for emails (allowance for multiple email accounts) with my custom domain instead of using an email client.

Last but not least, calling in as many favors from friends and acquaintances that are familiar with this technology and format. *(Editor, this is a key to success in any adventure: ask for help!)*

It was a very steep learning curve. New things I had to learn were:

Using "Zoom" to record my interviews

Lighting and green screen optimization

iMovie for video editing

Google suite and apple mail integration, spam avoidance, cross platform integration.

Google forms for automation and collation of speaker registrations.

Legal forms for speaker/expert agreements.

Fiverr to find freelancers to design graphics within budget.

How to find prospective guests for the summit

Reaching out/cold calling desired guests to participate

"Calendly" scheduling automation and integration with zoom and calendar.

The monster! Use, design, integration of Kartra (hosting platform) with:

Payment gateways (PayPal and stripe)

Main Website (Wix)

Email system and autoresponders (Google Suite, Gmail)

Notifications, categorisations, tags, leads, lists, etc.

External links and downloads

Page design

Marketing Copy writing

Organization of accounts in spreadsheets and online project management software (Trello)

"Canva" for flier, email attachments and Summit one page design

IT troubleshooting

Photo Editing

YouTube for creating subtitles

"Handbrake" for hardcoding Subtitles

Creating Transcripts

Social media automation (Hootsuite)

Affiliate management

How to conduct interviews

How to set up, follow up, organize and be professional on calls with prospective guests.

(editor, I'm tired just reading this, but the result was so worth it!)

I'm sure I have forgotten some. I am on my third summit now and still learning, still improving, and still creating more. The experience has been invaluable. Very hard work, but to be honest, it was so much fun as well.

I am grateful for this challenging time in the world as it forced me to "find another way", and I did, which gave me the opportunity to find something more aligned with who I am as a person than anything else I have done so far.

Keep learning, keep improving, keep energized....

Getting started is the first and most important step. The most important attitude is to be flexible.

Angelo Tirhas, *www.angelotirhas.com Included with permission*

Visit our resources page:
www.SuccessPublications.ca/PIVOT.html

A few final ideas from Bob...

If you want to achieve the 'mastery of the message' you will need to dig deep to master yourself first and then draw from that in preparing and delivering your message. **Applying the 3 M's will help you succeed.** (Message, Messenger, Method)

You owe it to your audiences to diligently prepare and to bring forth your best. Anything else would be a waste of everyone's time and energy.

Seeking to become a '*master of the message*' is the beginning of attaining the mastery – and the journey is worth it!

Use story starters to warm up your brain. To get you started, I've included some of my own story starters. These story starters give my brain a mental kick and get me thinking about something I might put into an easy format to capture and share an idea. Perhaps they will work for you too?

Ideas on using a 'How to' story starter:

How I learned the importance of _____:
How I got started in the _____ business.
My worse Customer Service experience: Why?
My favorite customer: why?
The best lesson I learned last year:
Something funny happened to me:
How to overcome _____:
How to initiate _____:
How to unravel the secret of _____:
My dream company: Why?
The best lesson I've learned here at _____:

Excerpt from Speaking for Success by **Bob 'Idea Man' Hooey**, *CVP, used with permission* www.ideaman.net

What they say about Bob 'Idea Man' Hooey

I frequently travel across North America, and more recently around the globe, sharing my **Ideas At Work!** With the advent of Covid-19, I pivoted to serve my clients online with virtual presentations. Now you can bring me in virtually.

I am fortunate to get feedback and comments from my audiences and colleagues.

These comments come from people who have been touched, challenged, or simply enjoyed themselves in one of my sessions around the globe.

"Thank you, Bob, it is always a pleasure to see a true professional at work. You have made the name 'Speaker' stand out as a truism — someone who encourages people to examine their lives and adjust. The comments indicated you hit people right where it is important — in their hearts. Each of those in your audience took away a new feeling of personal success and encouragement." **Sherry Knight**, Dimension Eleven Human Resources and Communications

"I am pleased to recommend Bob 'Idea Man' Hooey to any organization looking for a charismatic, confident speaker and seminar leader. I have seen Bob in action on several occasions, and he is ALWAYS on! Bob has the ability to grab his audience's attention and keep it. Quite simply, if Bob is involved — your program or seminar is guaranteed to succeed." **Maurice Laving**, Coordinator Training and Development, **London Drugs**

"On very short notice Bob cleared his schedule and graciously presented at our meeting when the original Speaker was unable to attend. **Last week Bob set the tone for our two-day BMO leadership meeting and gave us all a motivational lift.** *His compassion and true interest in people was clearly evident, making him very credible. He shared some great stories, has a wealth of experience and knowledge and it was a pleasure listening to him. His down-to-Earth style makes it easier to retain the information presented. He also followed up with additional info and handouts, cementing his message of building bridges, not walls. Fantastic job, Bob, and thanks again!"* **Barbara Afra Beler**, MBA, Senior Specialist Commercial Community, **Bank of Montreal**, Alberta North

"I still get comments from people about your presentation. Only a few speakers have left an impression that lasts that long. You hit a spot with the tourism people." **Janet Bell, Yukon Economic Forums**

"I have been so excited working with Bob Hooey, *as he has given inspiration and motivation to our leadership team members. Both at the Brick Warehouse – Alberta and at Art Van Furniture – Michigan; with his years of experience in working with business executives and his humorous and delightful packaging of his material, he makes* **learning with Bob a real joy.** *But most importantly, anyone who encounters his material is the better for it."*

Kim Yost, CEO Art Van Furniture (retired), former CEO The Brick

Please visit my friends who shared their ideas... let them know you appreciated their generosity in sharing from their experience. I am sure they will appreciate hearing from you.

Bob's Publications

Bob is a prolific author who has been capturing and sharing his wisdom and experience in printed and electronic forms for the past twenty plus years. In addition to the following publications he has written for consumer, corporate, professional associations, trade, and on-line publications.

He has also been engaged to write and assist on publications by other writers and companies.

Leadership, business, and career development series

Running TOO Fast (8th edition 2022)
Legacy of Leadership (6th edition 2024)
Make ME Feel Special! (6th edition 2022)
Why Didn't I 'THINK' of That? (5th edition 2022)
Speaking for Success! (10th edition 2023)
THINK Beyond the First Sale (3rd edition 2022)
Prepare Yourself to Win! (3rd edition 2017)
The early years… 1998-2009 – A Tip of the Hat collection
The saga continues… 2010-2019 - A Tip of the Hat collection (2023)

Bob's Mini-book success series

The Courage to Lead! (4th edition 2024)
Creative Conflict (3rd edition 2024)
THINK Before You Ink! (3rd edition 2017)
Running to Win! (2nd edition 2017)
Generate More Sales (5th edition 2023)
Unleash your Business Potential (3rd edition 2023)
Maximize Meetings (2024)

Learn to Listen (2nd edition 2023)
Creativity Counts! (2nd edition 2024)
Create Your Future! (3rd edition 2024)

Bob's Pocket Wisdom series

Pocket Wisdom for Speakers (updated 2019)
Pocket Wisdom for Leaders – Power of One! (2019)

Quick reads (2017-2020) - more to come in 2024

LEAD! *Idea-rich leadership success strategies*
CREATE! *Idea-rich strategies for enhanced innovation*
TIME! *Idea-rich tips for enhanced performance and productivity*
SERVE! *Idea-rich strategies for enhanced customer service*
SPEAK! *Idea-rich tips and techniques for great presentations*
CREATIVE CONFLICT *Idea-rich leadership for team success*
SUCCEED! *Idea-rich strategies to succeed in business, despite global disruptions (2020)*
WRITE ON! *Idea-rich tips and techniques to bring your book into pixels or print (2020)*
Get to Yes! *Idea-rich introductions to subtle art of creative persuasion in sales and negotiation (2020)*

Co-authored books created by Bob

Quantum Success – 3 volume series (2006)
In the Company of Leaders (95th anniversary Edition 2019)
Foundational Success (2nd Edition 2013)
PIVOT To Present: *Idea-rich strategies to deliver your virtual message with impact (2020)*

Visit: www.SuccessPublications.ca for more information

Copyright and License Notes

PIVOT To Present
Idea-rich strategies to deliver your virtual message with impact

Bob 'Idea Man' Hooey, Accredited Speaker, Certified Virtual Presenter, 2011 Spirit of CAPS recipient. Prolific author of 30 plus business, leadership, and career success publications. Author, Speaking for Success!

Photos of Bob: Bonnie-Jean McAllister,
www.elantraphotography.com
Dov Friedman, www.photographybyDov.com
Editorial, layout and design: **Irene Gaudet,** Vitrak Creative Services, vitrakcreative.com

Success Publications – a division of Creativity Corner Inc. Box 10, Egremont, AB T0A 0Z0 www.successpublications.ca Creative office: +1-780-736-0009

Acknowledgements and disclaimers

A very special dedication of this piece of myself, to the two people who meant the most to me, my folks Ron and Marge Hooey. Sadly, both my parents left this earthly realm in 1999. I still miss your encouragement and love. I was blessed with the two of you in my life.

*To my amazing wife and professional proof-reader, **Irene,** who loves, encourages, and supports me in my quest to continue sharing my **Ideas At Work!** across the world. Thank you seems so inadequate for your work in helping make my writing better!*

My thanks to the many people who have encouraged me in my growth as a leader, speaker, and engaging trainer in each area of expertise including sales and negotiation. My thanks to a select few friends for your ongoing support and constructive abuse. ☺ *You know who you are.*

Special thanks to each of my amazing colleagues and friends who have shared ideas, tips, techniques and lessons for this little book.

We have not attempted to cite in the electronic text all the authorities and sources consulted in the preparation of this manual. To do so would require much more space than is available. The list would include departments of various governments, libraries, industrial institutions, periodicals, and many individuals. Inspiration was drawn from many sources in the creation of this electronic text.

Warning—Disclaimer

This electronic book is written and designed to provide information on more effective sales and negotiation. It is sold with the explicit understanding that the publisher and author are <u>not</u> engaged in rendering legal, accounting, or other professional services. If legal or other expert assistance is required, the services of a competent professional in your geographic area should be sought.

It is not the purpose of this electronic book (manual) to reprint all the information that is otherwise available to sales professionals, negotiators, and sales leaders. Its primary purpose is to complement, amplify, and supplement other texts and reference materials. You are encouraged to search out and study all the available material, learn as much as possible, and tailor the information to your individual needs. This will help to enhance your success in being a more effective communicator online as well as sales leader, or business owner.

*Every effort has been made to make this electronic 'primer' as complete and as accurate as possible within the scope of its focus. However, there **may be mistakes**, both typographical and in content. Therefore, this electronic text should be used only as a general guide or primer and not as the ultimate source of information. Furthermore, this electronic manual contains information that is current only up to the date of publication.*

The purpose of this 'primer' is to educate and entertain; perhaps to inform and to inspire. The author(s), contributors and/ or publisher shall have <u>neither</u> liability <u>nor</u> responsibility to any person or entity with respect to any loss or damage caused, or alleged to have been caused, directly or indirectly, by the information contained in this electronic 'primer' manual or electronic book.

Visit our resources page:
<u>www.SuccessPublications.ca/ PIVOT.html</u>

A final note: With the pandemic abated, we are free to move around the globe. Still, on-line is here to stay and is a part of our tool box going forward.

Thanks for reading PIVOT To Present

Each time I sit down to write, or in this case compile, edit, and write, I am challenged to ensure I deliver something that will be of use-it-now value to my reader.

I think we did here.

I ask myself, **"If I was reading this, what would I be looking for?"** As well as **"Why is this relevant to me, today?"**

These two questions help to keep me focused, help me to remain clear on my objectives; and they help to remind me to dig into my experiences, stories, examples, and research to provide solid information that will be of benefit and help my readers, when they apply it, succeed. **PIVOT To Present** is my attempt to capture some of the valuable lessons learned over the past 25 plus years, and virtually in the past 6 months, and to share them with you. And to share lessons from 26 amazing colleagues who have successfully pivoted to present on-line.

Bob 'Idea Man' Hooey
www.ideaman.net
www.SuccessPublications.ca
www.HaveMouthWillTravel.com

Connect with me on:
Facebook: http://www.facebook.com/bob.hooey
LinkedIn: www.linkedin.com/in/canadianideamanbobhooey
YouTube: www.youtube.com/ideamanbob
Smashwords: www.smashwords.com/profile/view/Hooey